Barbecues

SALADS AND PICNICS

PHOTOGRAPHY BY ROWAN FOTHERINGHAM
STYLING BY DONNA HAY

BayBooks

An imprint of HarperCollins*Publishers*

STOCKISTS

Accoutrement Cook Shop
611 Military Road
Mosman NSW
Tel: (02) 969 1031
(also Lemongrove, Chatswood)

Country Road Homewear
427 Victoria Road
Chatswood NSW
Tel: (02) 413 3754
(stores all over Australia)

Hale Imports
Pillivuyt
97–99 Old Pittwater Road
Brookvale NSW
Tel: (02) 938 2400

Les Olivades
2 Transvaal Ave
Double Bay NSW
Tel: (02) 327 8073

Orrefors Kosta Boda
Shop 1033 Westfield Shopping Centre
Miranda
Tel: (02) 524 9409
(also Frenchs Forest, Mosman)

A BAY BOOKS PUBLICATION
Bay Books, an imprint of
HarperCollins*Publishers*
25 Ryde Road, Pymble, Sydney NSW 2073, Australia
31 View Road, Glenfield, Auckland 10, New Zealand

First published in Australia in 1993

Copyright © Bay Books 1993

National Library of Australia
Cataloguing-in-Publication data:
  Hay, Donna.
    Barbecues, picnics & salads.
    Includes index.
    ISBN 1 86378 086 6.
    1. Barbecue cookery. 2. Salads. 3. Picnicking. I. Title. (Series: Bay Books country-style cookery).
  641.578

Cover, chapter openers and some internal photography by Rowan Fotheringham
Food stylist: Donna Hay
Food stylist's assistant: Beth Pitman

Front cover photograph: Greek Brochettes (recipe page 25), Red Mullet in Corn Husks (recipe page 34)
Back cover photograph: Lobster with Cress and Balsamic Vinegar (recipe page 39)
Bowls from Orrefors Kosta Boda

Printed by Griffin Press, Adelaide
Printed in Australia

9 8 7 6 5 4 3 2 1
97 96 95 94 93

CONTENTS

4

EATING OUTDOORS

8

BRILLIANT BARBECUES

Fire Starters
Serving with Sizzle
Breads and Spreads

52

IN THE SHADE OF THE GARDEN

58

PORTABLE PICNICS

70

SOMETHING ON THE SIDE

Salads
Dash or Splash

88

TABLES: SALAD VEGETABLES,
SALAD GREENS

93

MEASUREMENTS AND GLOSSARY

94

INDEX

Eating Outdoors

What better way to enjoy the great outdoors than to barbecue a feast, entertain guests in the garden or pack a picnic. *Barbecues, Picnics and Salads* is packed with recipe ideas for all these occasions.

BARBECUE PERFECTION

To barbecue simply means to cook over an open fire. Over millenia, since fire was discovered, people have built some sort of fireplace to cook food — especially meat or fish. Today, barbecues are more popular than ever. The only problem is in choosing which kind best suits your needs.

Which Barbecue?

Barbecues come in many types and sizes ranging from the most basic firebowls to those with the latest features. Work out exactly what you want your barbecue for — decide on the size for your needs and whether you need a portable or a fixed one — set yourself a price limit and the rest should be plain sailing.

WHAT KIND OF BARBECUE? What do you plan to use your barbecue for? Obviously it is not worth investing in the top-of-the-range trolley barbecue if you eat outdoors only a couple of times a year. On the other hand, if you entertain frequently, it is equally poor value to buy a barbecue that's too small or flimsy and won't last the distance.

PORTABLE OR FIXED? A permanent barbecue is great if you entertain often or eat outdoors regularly; but it needs to be positioned for summer shade and winter sun. A portable barbecue — such as a smaller rectangular or bowl-shaped one — has the advantage that you can use it both for picnics and in your garden. You can also move it around to take advantage of the sun.

TYPE Grills, hotplate or covered? If you simply want to barbecue on the grill then the widest range of barbecues is available, from the basic hibachi to a top-of-the-range trolley with all the features you can imagine. A hotplate can be useful for onions or eggs, and many models combine both cooking surfaces. If you plan to entertain adventurously then you may want a rotisserie for spit-roasting. The increasingly popular covered barbecues, which can be used with the lid up for barbecuing, or closed for roasting and even smoking, lets you cook in the great outdoors in all weathers.

SIZE Make sure that the cooking area is large enough for your needs. It is better to buy a little too big than too small as it is important to be able to serve everyone together when eating alfresco. Trolley barbecues are increasingly popular because they come in a range of sizes and most provide some preparation space as well.

Fuel

WOOD Traditionally used for cooking in the great outdoors, wood is not the best fuel for barbecuing because it burns with a flame. Barbecue cooking needs heat — not flames. It is essential to let flames die down leaving a bed of red hot embers before cooking. All too often people light the fire and start barbecuing. We all know the rather charred results.

CHARCOAL Charcoal is essentially wood that has already been burnt down. This greatly speeds up the process of turning your fuel into a glowing bed of heat. It is the most effective fuel for barbecuing because:
• it provides plenty of heat,

- it is ready for cooking over in 15 to 20 minutes,
- there's no smell,
- it can be bought in bags from department and hardware stores, and
- fatty flare-ups are not a problem because you can 'damp' to control the temperature.

BARBECUE FUEL Barbecue fuels such as heat beads are popular for barbecuing because they can be bought in conveniently sized bags and provide good heat for relatively long periods of time. Like charcoal, they have less tendency to flare up than wood. However, they are harder to light and you can not use the damping technique as successfully. They take about 30 to 40 minutes to reach the cooking stage. Because heat beads burn away to a very fine ash, place them on a steel sheet or a fine grate — otherwise you will find they tend to fall through.

GAS Gas barbecues tend to be more expensive but their big attraction is obviously their convenience: you can start barbecuing almost immediately. With the introduction of volcanic rock, gas barbecues have become even more popular. The rock is spread out below the cooking surface, absorbing the heat from the burners and glowing just like charcoal or heat beads. This not only spreads the heat over a larger area but gives food an authentic barbecue flavour. Gas barbecues just couldn't be easier to operate: you simply connect the gas bottle and turn on. It is always a good idea to keep a spare bottle in case

the gas runs out. However, you can't use the damping technique to 'moisturise' food while cooking unless the burners are protected by a metal shield.

ELECTRICITY Electric barbecues are great for people living in apartment buildings. But they do have limited application because of the necessary power points and leads. Electric barbecues can also be combined with volcanic rock for that more authentic flavour.

Other Features to Consider

STABILITY It is essential to buy a barbecue that stands squarely on the ground. The top-of-the-range trolleys provide the maximum stability in portables, but they are also the most expensive. Smaller portables or portables with detachable or fold-away legs tend to be less stable. Check the angle of the legs and overall stability before you buy. Table models need to be looked at with the same care, although most have very short legs or supports, and are quite stable.

COOKING HEIGHT Many barbecues have the cooking surface too close to the coals — we recommend that it should be at least 25 to 40 cm above the source of the heat. A barbecue with an adjustable height cooking surface is probably a good buy.

MATERIALS If your barbecue lives outdoors, make sure it is made of materials that won't rust away too readily. Alternatively, invest in a cover or put the portable barbecue in the garden shed.

SHELVES From the can of beer to food and sauces, you need plenty of space for putting things when barbecuing. Extra space never goes amiss, but a table alongside will do the trick. Warming racks above the barbecue are also useful, but not essential.

Barbecue Cooking Techniques

There are a variety of ways to cook a barbecue, from grilling, the most popular technique, through to spit-roasting. Try wrapping vegetables in foil and putting them in the hot embers to cook, or cooking shellfish in their shells — it's delicious!

BARBECUING Barbecue grilling or cooking food on a grill over the heat remains the most popular technique. Most of us have fond memories of succulent pieces of steak on the barbecue grill. The basic principles are to cook with heat, not flames, and retain the natural juices inside the food. Turning constantly allows the juices that run under heat to baste the food naturally. Any juices and fat which do drip fall on the fire, vaporise, and are absorbed back in the meat, adding a flavour which is unique to food barbecued in this way.

It doesn't take long to barbecue foods that are up to 5 cm thick and lie flat on the barbecue, or which can be cooked in wire barbecue baskets. Larger pieces of meat can be barbecued on the grill but need to be turned constantly and watched carefully so that the outside does not burn during the longer cooking time required.

The damping technique, plus constant turning, ensures that food is juicy when cooked. Don't overcook. Remember that your meat, fish or poultry will continue cooking in its own heat when taken off the barbecue. So remove just before it's ready.

DAMPING

Damping is essential for successful barbecuing. Damp the fire with water either from a very fine spray on your hose or by carefully sprinkling or squirting about a cup of water over the coals. This not only decreases the temperature immediately but it puts moisture back into the food with rising steam. If your barbecue grill is rather close to the coals you may wish to move the food aside as you spray or sprinkle.

Do not damp down a gas barbecue unless there is a steel shield covering the burners.

HOTPLATE With hotplate cooking it is the heat of the plate that cooks food rather than the direct heat of the fire. A thick plate will take longer to heat up, but will hold the heat longer than a thin one. It will also be less affected by the changes in the fire underneath, but consequently less responsive.

Essentially, using a hotplate means that you are frying your food. It is most important to have good drainage for the fat and not underestimate how much there will be. Good drainage eliminates the risk of fat running on the fire, or building up and virtually deep-frying the food. If you want to fry onions or eggs on your barbecue a frypan will do the job just as well.

FOIL Vegetables in foil are popular — particularly potatoes and corn. Use heavy-duty foil or two layers and wrap food with the dull side of the foil on the outside. Place parcels on the grill and turn while cooking. Potatoes are great when wrapped in foil and placed in the embers.

SKEWERS Everything from meat, poultry and fish to fruit or vegetables can be cooked kebab-style on skewers. Cut meat into same-sized pieces. Remember, with beef or lamb kebabs, cook them later for those who like them rare.

The type of skewers you use is important: choose flat ones with a diamond-shaped end so that the food will stay on the skewer and will not roll around when turned.

Kebab turners come battery-operated so you don't have to do a thing when cooking. Alternatively, there are kebab holders that support the skewers and you turn by hand as required.

ROTISSERIE Rotisserie cooking, or spit-roasting, is a visually entertaining way to barbecue food but it takes a long time. A whole bird, for example, is threaded on a metal spit which is then turned slowly over the fire. Rotisseries can be simple hand-turned varieties or modern battery-operated units which are much more convenient. Apart from turning, little attention is needed during cooking, though you may like to brush with a baste from about halfway through cooking time. Spit-roasting a 1.5 kg chicken would take 1½ hours.

To speed up cooking time and ensure even cooking, fit reflectors to the sides of the barbecue at the height of the food. To prevent flare-ups, place a drip tray directly under the meat to catch the fat. COVERED BARBECUES Barbecues with a lid are more like an outdoor oven enabling you to bake, grill and smoke food. You adjust the dampers to increase or reduce the temperature or maintain the required heat.

GOURMET GARDEN DINING

What better way to enjoy a meal than in your own garden. All you need is some comfortable garden furniture and you're all set. Make sure you put your table and chairs in the shade for those hot summer days.

Eating in the garden at night in the fresh night air is also a treat — light the table with candles for a pleasing effect.

Once you are all set up, turn to our delicious recipes for garden meals and whip up a feast.

PACKING A PICNIC

These days going on a picnic is easy with the modern day picnic sets that come with all sorts of useful utensils and containers. However, you don't need to rush out and buy a picnic set — most of us have everything we need at home. Of course a picnic basket does come in handy to carry everything to the picnic spot, particularly if it's far from the car! Don't forget to take a blanket, and a plastic bag for rubbish is a good idea.

It's best to take nonbreakable plates, cups and glasses as these can be stacked with no fear of damage. Always rinse if possible before packing back into the hamper at the end of the picnic or it will be a mess by the time you get home.

It's important to take food that is easy to pack, easy to eat and easy to put away to go home, so it may be best to forget anything that's very saucy or greasy. Pack all food in containers that don't leak.

Sandwiches of course are the ever useful, versatile and non-messy picnic food and with some imagination even these can be creative. Savoury pastries, tartlets and pies are always good as well as cold meats and nibbles like olives and sun-dried tomatoes. Take breads and crackers with dips (in tightly sealed containers) and salads are always great to pick at, but keep the dressing in a jar until you are ready to eat. For dessert, cakes are always good, but slices, muffins and biscuits may be easier to pass around. Watch out for the ants.

For drinks, wine and beer are always popular and of course, fruit juice and water for the kids. If you have an esky or cooler box, all the better!

In our chapter *Portable Picnics* you will find irresistible recipes for a perfect picnic.

SUPER SALADS

The boring garden salad with lettuce, tomato and cucumber is a thing of the past. Salads can be creative, delicious combinations of all sorts of vegetables and other ingredients. They can also be terribly simple — try combining three or four kinds of lettuce with some chopped fresh herbs and a special vinaigrette dressing of your choice. The salads in our chapter *Something on the Side* will give you ideas to create your own and the recipes for dressings and mayonnaises will convert any salad into something special.

All you need for a successful salad is fresh ingredients, and the rest is easy. A perfect meal for a summer's day could be made out of lots of salads with some crusty, hearty breads. So simple and so healthy. See our section on salad greens and vegetables on pages 88 to 92.

Brilliant Barbecues

*B*arbecues are a traditional way of cooking food out-of-doors, and while they can be simple and easy, they have also developed into a more formal way of presenting food. Marinades can transform a plain steak into something special and with today's awareness of eating healthily, seafood is enjoying a new lease of life on the barbecue. Yet what could be more relaxing, or enjoyable, than entertaining guests who come and chat to the cook over the coals?

Plate from Pillivuyt, glasses from Orrefors Kosta Boda

Fire Starters

Don't keep your guests starving while the meat's on the barbecue: serve up some of these delicious starters, many of which can be prepared in advance. There are spreads, pâtés, curry puffs and meatballs, to name a few.

OYSTER CHEESE PUFFS

125 g (4 oz) butter

1½ cups (185 g) grated tasty cheese

2 teaspoons sherry

1 egg, separated

210 g (7 oz) canned smoked oysters, drained

32 x 4 cm (2 in) bread rounds

1 tablespoon finely chopped fresh parsley

paprika, to taste

Beat butter, cheese and sherry together. Add egg yolk and beat well. Whisk egg white until soft peaks form. Fold egg white into cheese mixture.

Place 1 oyster onto each round of bread. Top with a teaspoonful of cheese mixture. Sprinkle with chopped parsley and paprika. Place on oven trays. Bake at 230°C (450°F) for 10 minutes and serve piping hot.

MAKES 32

CHIVE AND PECAN CHEESE ROUNDS

155 g (5 oz) ricotta cheese

155 g (5 oz) vintage cheddar, finely grated

½ teaspoon freshly ground black pepper

1 tablespoon chopped fresh chives

½ teaspoon chilli powder

¾ cup (90 g/3 oz) finely chopped pecan nuts

Place ricotta, cheddar, pepper, chives and chilli powder in a small bowl. Mix well to combine.

Cover mixture with plastic wrap and refrigerate until firm. Shape into 2 small rounds and roll in pecan nuts. Serve with small rounds of crusty bread.

SERVES 2 TO 4

CHOPPING CHIVES

An easy way to chop chives is to snip them with sharp scissors. The whole stem can be used.
The flowers make a very attractive garnish.

Picture previous pages: Roasted Capsicum Dip (page 22), Warm Salad of Barbecued Beef and Radicchio (page 37), Pear and Blue Brie Chicken (page 33)

CHEESE AND PORT SPREAD

90 g (3 oz) butter, softened

125 g (4 oz) creamy blue vein cheese

125 g (4 oz) smoked cheese, finely grated

½ tablespoon port

½ teaspoon white pepper

Place butter, blue vein and smoked cheese in a small bowl and beat until smooth.

Mix through port and pepper.

Spoon into serving dish and chill until required.

SERVES 8

Chive and Pecan Cheese Rounds, Cheese and Port Spread

SALMON AND CHIVE LOG

220 g (7 oz) cream cheese

2 tablespoons sour cream

1 tablespoon fresh lemon juice

3 spring onions, chopped

2 bunches chives, finely chopped

420 g (14 oz) canned red salmon, drained and boned

1 teaspoon freshly ground black pepper

⅓ cup (40 g/1½ oz) chopped pecan nuts

Place cream cheese, sour cream and lemon juice in a bowl and beat until smooth.

Fold spring onions, a quarter of the chives, salmon and pecan nuts through cream cheese mixture. Refrigerate mixture until firm.

Place mixture on a sheet of plastic wrap and shape into a log. Roll the cheese log in remaining chives and refrigerate until needed. Serve with crackers or bread.

SERVES 4 TO 6

COCONUT CURRY PUFFS

2 teaspoons oil

1 onion, chopped

2 cloves garlic, crushed

500 g (1 lb) minced beef

1 tablespoon curry paste

1 tablespoon chopped coriander

1 red chilli, chopped

1 potato, grated

1 cup (250 ml/8 fl oz) coconut milk

1 kg (2 lb) ready-rolled puff pastry

1 egg, lightly beaten

oil for frying

Heat oil in a large fry pan, add onion, garlic and beef, and sauté until brown. Add curry paste, coriander, chilli, potato and coconut milk.

Simmer for 8 minutes or until mixture is thick. Allow to cool.

Cut pastry into 6 cm (2½ in) rounds. Place a spoonful of filling onto each round. Brush edges of pastry with egg and press to seal. Deep fry in hot oil until golden.

MAKES 15

Coconut Curry Puffs

SALMON AND LIME PATE

880 g (1¾ lb) canned salmon, drained and bones removed

1 large cucumber, peeled, seeded and chopped

2 spring onions, chopped

2 tablespoons lime juice

2 teaspoons grated lime rind

½ cup (125 ml/4 fl oz) mayonnaise

2 teaspoons French mustard

1 tablespoon gelatine dissolved in 3 tablespoons boiling water

Place salmon, cucumber, spring onions, lime juice and rind, mayonnaise and mustard in a food processor or blender and process until smooth.

Stir gelatine mixture through salmon mixture. Pour mixture into a lightly oiled mould. Cover and chill for 4 hours or until set.

SERVES 8 TO 10

SPICY SKEWERED MEATBALLS

....

500 g (1 lb) minced beef

1 onion, finely chopped

1 egg, lightly beaten

1 cup (60 g/2 oz) fresh breadcrumbs

2 tablespoons tomato sauce

2 tablespoons sweet chilli sauce

1 teaspoon ground cumin

1 tablespoon chopped fresh parsley

Spicy Skewered Meatballs

Place beef, onion, egg, breadcrumbs, tomato sauce, chilli sauce, cumin and parsley in a bowl and mix well to combine.

Roll mixture into small balls. Place 2 meatballs on each skewer and barbecue or grill, turning frequently for 10 minutes or until cooked. Serve with a spicy dipping sauce.

MAKES 18

BALSAMIC SMOKED BEEF ROUNDS

12 small slices bread

¼ cup (125 ml/4 fl oz) sour cream

½ teaspoon horseradish cream

1 teaspoon grain mustard

12 slices smoked beef

1 tablespoon balsamic vinegar

cracked black pepper

1 tablespoon small basil leaves

Spread bread slices with combined sour cream, horseradish and mustard.

Top with smoked beef, sprinkle with balsamic vinegar, pepper and basil.

SERVES 6

HERB PANCAKES WITH AVOCADO BUTTER

½ cup (60 g/2 oz) plain flour, sifted

½ cup (60 g/2 oz) self-raising flour, sifted

1 egg, lightly beaten

½ cup (125 ml/4 fl oz) milk

20 g (¾ oz) chopped fresh mixed herbs

1 teaspoon cracked black pepper

AVOCADO BUTTER

½ avocado

60 g (2 oz) butter

1 tablespoon fresh lemon or lime juice

½ teaspoon cracked pepper

Place flours, egg, milk, herbs and pepper in a small bowl and whisk until smooth.

Pour spoonfuls of batter onto a hot greased barbecue plate or frypan.

Herb Pancakes with Avocado Butter, Balsamic Smoked Beef Rounds

Cook until golden brown on both sides. Keep warm.

To Make Avocado Butter: Place avocado, butter, lemon juice and pepper in a small bowl and mix until smooth. Spread on top of pancakes and serve.

SERVES 8 TO 10

MUSHROOM AND HAM PASTRIES

4 sheets frozen ready-rolled puff pastry, thawed

1 egg, beaten

FILLING

125 g (4 oz) ham, diced

1 onion, chopped

125 g (4 oz) mushrooms, sliced

30 g (1 oz) butter

1 stick celery, chopped

1 tablespoon chopped fresh parsley

2 teaspoons tomato purée or paste

freshly ground black pepper, to taste

Fry ham, onion and mushrooms in butter until onion is transparent. Add celery, parsley, tomato purée and pepper. Heat until liquid has evaporated. Remove from heat and cool.

Cut pastry sheets into 9 rounds, using a 10 cm (4 in) cutter. Place a tablespoon of mixture on one half of each round. Fold over pastry to form half moon shape. Press edges together to seal, and use prongs of a fork for decoration. Brush with beaten egg.

Place pastries on baking tray. Bake at 220°C (420°F) for 15 to 20 minutes. Serve hot or cold.

MAKES 36

Prawns with Creamy Cashew Nut Sauce

PREPARING PRAWNS (SHRIMPS)

Cut off the head, remove the tail and shell. Use a sharp knife to devein them. Prawns are cooked when they are red.

PRAWNS WITH CREAMY CASHEW NUT SAUCE

½ cup (60 g/2 oz) finely chopped cashew nuts

1 clove garlic, crushed

2 tablespoons light soy sauce

1 teaspoon grated lemon rind

1 red chilli, chopped

½ cup (125 ml/4 fl oz) cream

2 teaspoons cornflour blended with 1 tablespoon water

1 kg (2 lb) uncooked prawns (shrimps), shelled, deveined with tails on

Place cashew nuts, garlic, soy, lemon rind, chilli, cream and cornflour mixture in a small pan. Stir over a low heat until mixture thickens.

Thread prawns onto skewers and barbecue or grill, basting frequently with sauce. Serve with remaining sauce.

SERVES 6 TO 8

SMOKED TROUT TARTLETS

1 loaf sliced white bread

60 g (2 oz) butter, melted

FILLING

1 smoked trout (about 300 g/ 9½ oz), skinned and boned

3 tablespoons mayonnaise

2 spring onions, finely chopped

1 tablespoon chopped chives

1 teaspoon horseradish cream

1 teaspoon mustard

1 teaspoon freshly ground black pepper

black olives, pitted and cut into strips

Preheat oven to 100°C (200°F).

Trim crusts from bread and flatten with a rolling pin. Brush both sides with butter and press into tartlet tins. Bake for 10 minutes or until crisp and golden. Cool.

To Prepare Filling: Place trout in a small bowl and break flesh into small pieces with a fork. Add mayonnaise, spring onions, chives, horseradish, mustard and pepper and mix well.

Spoon trout filling into tart cases, garnish with strips of olives and serve immediately.

MAKES 34

KEBABS

Flat, metal skewers with an insulated handle are best for kebabs on the barbecue. If you are using bamboo satay sticks, soak them in water beforehand. You could also make some hairpin style skewers. Bend stainless steel wire into hairpin-shaped skewers about 20 cm (8 in) long and 1½ cm (½ in) wide.

CHEESE AND OLIVE MELTS

These are great to make whilst the barbecue is heating up to its full potential.

12 slices olive bread

½ cup (60 g/2 oz) grated smoked cheese

½ cup (60 g/2 oz) grated Swiss cheese

⅓ cup (60 g/2 oz) chopped olives

1 tablespoon thyme leaves

Place 2 slices of olive bread onto a piece of foil. Sprinkle with smoked cheese, Swiss cheese, olives and thyme. Seal foil package. Repeat with remaining ingredients.

Place on a warm barbecue and cook for 4 to 5 minutes or until cheese is warm and melted. These can also be cooked under a hot grill until golden and cheese is bubbling.

SERVES 6

Smoked Trout Tartlets

PEPPERED CHICKEN PATE

* 500 g (1 lb) chicken livers, trimmed
* 1 onion, chopped
* 2 cloves garlic, crushed
* 250 g (8 oz) unsalted butter
* 1 tablespoon chopped fresh sage
* 2 tablespoons chopped fresh basil
* 2 teaspoons freshly ground black pepper
* 2 tablespoons brandy
* fresh bay leaves
* 90 g (3 oz) clarified butter, melted

Roughly chop livers and add to a hot pan with onion, garlic and 60 g (2 oz) of the butter. Sauté this mixture until livers are lightly cooked and onion is soft.

Place liver mixture, herbs (except for bay leaves), remaining butter, pepper and brandy into a food processor or blender and process until smooth.

Pour mixture into a terrine or serving dish and chill until slightly set. Arrange bay leaves on top of pâté. Pour over clarified butter and chill until set.

SERVES 6 TO 8

Peppered Chicken Pâté

Clarified butter, also called ghee, is butter-fat with the milk solids and salt removed. It can be heated to greater temperatures than fresh butter without burning and is therefore often used for frying, especially in Indian cooking. It also imparts a different flavour and colour to fresh butter. It can be purchased from the supermarket in cartons and should be stored in an airtight container. It will keep refrigerated for many months and in cooler climates will keep unrefrigerated for many weeks. You can make your own clarified butter by heating fresh butter gently until a foam forms on the top. Cook a few seconds more then remove from heat. A milky residue will sink to the bottom, leaving the clear clarified butter on the top. Pour this into another container.

BARBECUE BRUSCHETTA

These can be made while standing around the barbecue or on the stove inside. Either way these simple nibbles are very easy and a definite crowd pleaser.

BASIC BRUSCHETTA

* 12 small slices of crusty bread
* 2 tablespoons olive oil
* 2 cloves garlic, halved

Brush both sides of bread with olive oil. Place on barbecue or under grill until both sides are golden brown.

Rub toasted bread with garlic and serve plain or with any of the following toppings.

SERVES 6

TOMATO, SAGE AND RED ONION

* 2 tomatoes, chopped
* 1 tablespoon chopped sage leaves
* 1 red onion, finely sliced
* 1 teaspoon cracked black pepper

Place tomato, sage, red onion and pepper on barbecue plate or in a pan and toss until mixture is soft. Pile on top of bruschetta and serve warm.

MUSHROOM AND CAPSICUM

* 200 g (7 oz) small button mushrooms, halved
* ½ red capsicum (pepper), chopped
* ½ yellow capsicum (pepper), chopped
* 2 tablespoons chopped fresh basil
* 1 teaspoon cracked black pepper

Place mushrooms, capsicums, basil and pepper on barbecue or in a pan. Sauté for 3 to 4 minutes, then serve on top of bruschetta.

ZUCCHINI AND FETTA

* 2 zucchini (courgettes) thinly sliced
* 6 sun-dried tomatoes, chopped
* 200 g (7 oz) fetta, chopped

Place zucchini, tomatoes and fetta on barbecue or in a pan. Cook for 3 to 4 minutes or until heated through. Serve on top of bruschetta.

MEDITERRANEAN OYSTERS

24 oysters in the shell

3 tablespoons balsamic vinegar

6 slices prosciutto, chopped

cracked black pepper

Preheat grill.

Sprinkle oysters with balsamic vinegar. Top with pieces of prosciutto and pepper.

Place under grill for 1 minute or until prosciutto is crisp.

SERVES 4 TO 6

HONEYED PRAWNS

1 kg (2 lb) cooked large prawns (shrimps), shelled and deveined

MARINADE

1 cup (250 ml/8 fl oz) dark honey

1 cup (250 ml/8 fl oz) tomato sauce

½ cup (125 ml/4 fl oz) olive oil

freshly ground black pepper

1 tablespoon dry mustard

dash Tabasco sauce

Combine marinade ingredients in a bowl and blend well. Marinate prawns 15 to 30 minutes then thread 2 to 3 prawns on each skewer and barbecue over a good hot fire. Brush with remaining marinade and turn. Barbecue time about 5 to 6 minutes.

SERVES 6 TO 8

CHAR-GRILLED BABY OCTOPUS WITH PESTO MAYONNAISE

1 kg (2 lb) baby octopus, cleaned and halved

1 clove garlic, crushed

2 tablespoons brown sugar

½ cup (125 ml/4 fl oz) red wine

1 tablespoon lemon thyme leaves

PESTO MAYONNAISE

½ cup (125 ml/4 fl oz) whole egg mayonnaise

¼ cup (125 ml/4 fl oz) ready-made pesto

Place octopus, garlic, sugar, wine and thyme in a bowl and marinate for 1 to 2 hours.

Cook on a hot barbecue plate, tossing regularly until octopus is cooked and tender.

To Make Pesto Mayonnaise: Mix together mayonnaise and pesto. Serve with octopus as a dip or spoon over as a sauce.

SERVES 8 TO 10

MARINADE FOR OCTOPUS

A very simple way to barbecue octopus is to marinade it in a mixture of olive oil, fresh lemon juice, crushed garlic and fresh parsley. After cleaning the octopus, brush with marinade and barbecue for 10 minutes. The octopus will curl and then turn a claret red colour which looks very attractive in a garlic salad. If octopus is tough, tenderise before cooking by steaming for about 4 to 5 minutes.

Mediterranean Oysters, Char-grilled Baby Octopus with Pesto Mayonnaise

ROASTED CAPSICUM DIP

3 red capsicums (peppers)
2 tablespoons tomato paste
2 spring onions, chopped
1 tablespoon shredded basil
1 tablespoon balsamic vinegar
150 g (5 oz) cream cheese
1 teaspoon cracked black pepper

Preheat grill.

Halve capsicums and remove seeds; flatten slightly. Place under grill and cook until skins are charred and black. Place capsicums in a plastic bag and cool for 5 minutes. Peel away charred skins.

Finely chop two-thirds of the roasted capsicums and place in a bowl with tomato paste, spring onions, basil, and balsamic vinegar.

Place remaining capsicum and cream cheese in a blender or food processor and process until smooth. Fold into tomato mixture with pepper. Serve chilled with crisp toasts or vegetables.

SERVES 4 TO 6

SESAME DRUMSTICKS

8 chicken legs
3 tablespoons seasoned flour
1 egg, lightly beaten
3 tablespoons milk
3 tablespoons sesame seeds

3 tablespoons fresh breadcrumbs
60 g (2 oz) butter, melted

Preheat oven to 180°C (350°F).

Dust chicken lightly in flour. Dip into combined egg and milk. Roll in combined sesame seeds and breadcrumbs.

Place chicken legs in a greased baking dish and bake for 30 minutes.

Brush chicken with butter and return to oven and bake for a further 15 minutes or until cooked. Serve hot or cold.

SERVES 6 TO 8

Sesame Drumsticks

MARINATED BOCCONCINI

½ cup (125 ml/4 fl oz) olive oil

sprigs of fresh herbs (thyme, dill, basil, tarragon)

2 teaspoons cracked black pepper

6 to 8 bocconcini

Place oil, herbs and pepper in a small saucepan and heat until oil is warm. Keep oil at a low temperature for 5 minutes.

Remove pan from heat and allow to cool completely.

Place bocconcini in a clean glass jar. Pour over oil, seal and place in the refrigerator. Allow to stand for 2 days before serving.

SERVES 6 TO 8

Marinated Bocconcini

BOCCONCINI

Bocconcini is a small, white, soft, moist mildly sweet cheese. Bocconcini should only be bought when required. It can be stored in a cold refrigerator for up to 3 weeks but it will ripen and become firm and dry. If it goes yellow it should not be used.

Serving with Sizzle

Barbecuing can be far more tantalising than steak and sausages. Here are a variety of recipes for beef, lamb, chicken, fish, lobster and shellfish to serve as the main course at a barbecue. Many of these involve marinades so make sure you prepare them in plenty of time before the barbecue.

CHAR-GRILLED BEEF WITH AVOCADO AND TOMATOES

4 beef steaks (fillet or rump)

2 cloves garlic, crushed

2 teaspoons cracked black pepper

1 avocado, sliced

8 sun-dried tomatoes, sliced

1 tablespoon shredded basil

Trim steaks of any visible fat or sinew. Sprinkle steaks with garlic and pepper.

Place steaks on a hot char-grill or barbecue and cook for 3 to 4 minutes.

Turn steaks and top cooked side with avocado slices, tomatoes and basil. The topping will become warm whilst the other side is cooking.

Finish cooking steaks to your liking and serve with a mixed lettuce salad.

SERVES 4

GREEK BROCHETTES

500 g (1 lb) lean lamb, cubed

200 g (7 oz) pitted black olives

300 g (10 oz) goat's cheese or fetta cheese, cubed

250 g (8 oz) cherry tomatoes

2 tablespoons olive oil

2 tablespoons chopped fresh thyme

2 teaspoons grated lemon rind

2 teaspoons cracked black pepper

Thread lamb, olives, cheese and cherry tomatoes onto metal skewers.

Place oil, thyme, lemon and pepper in a small bowl and mix to combine.

Brush over brochettes and barbecue until tender, turning frequently and brushing with thyme baste.

SERVES 4

EASY FOOD PREPARATION

Try to prepare as much food as possible in advance. Choose foods that can remain in the refrigerator or freezer for a few days, so that once the guests arrive, only the barbecue items are left to cook.

Char-grilled Beef with Avocado and Tomatoes, Greek Brochettes

SPICY FISH KEBABS

1 kg (2 lb) firm white fish fillets

MARINADE

2 cloves garlic, crushed

⅔ cup (160 ml/5 fl oz) plain yoghurt

1 teaspoon chopped fresh ginger

1 red chilli, finely chopped

2 teaspoons garam marsala

1 tablespoon chopped fresh coriander

Cut fish fillets into 3 cm (1 in) cubes.

To Make Marinade: Place garlic, yoghurt, ginger, chilli, garam masala and coriander in a small bowl and mix to combine.

Thread fish cubes onto skewers. Spoon yoghurt marinade over fish and refrigerate for 1 hour.

Grill or barbecue skewers for 5 to 6 minutes. Serve with flat bread and salad.

SERVES 6

BUYING MEAT

Cheaper cross cuts don't suddenly become top quality on the barbecue. Buy good meat. Don't spoil the good feeling that you get from the great outdoors with cheap meat. Good meat is good value. There's no waste because it's all eaten.
When buying lamb always look for choice cuts, which should be pinkish red in colour. The flesh should be of a fine grained texture, and the fat, firm and pinkish white. With mutton, the flesh is more grainy in texture.

LIME AND PEPPER PRAWNS

1 kg (2 lb) green prawns (shrimps), shelled and deveined with tails left intact

3 cloves garlic, crushed

1 tablespoon cracked black pepper

1 to 2 red chillies, finely chopped

½ cup (125 ml/4 fl oz) lime juice

1 tablespoon lime rind strips

2 tablespoons butter

Place prawns, garlic, pepper, chillies, lime juice and rind in a bowl and toss to combine. Cover and refrigerate for 2 to 3 hours.

Place butter on a hot barbecue and heat until bubbling. Add prawns and marinade to barbecue and toss for 2 to 3 minutes or until prawns change colour.

SERVES 4 TO 6

HONEY LAMB SKEWERS

1 kg (2 lb) lean lamb, diced

2 onions, cut into wedges

MARINADE

3 tablespoons dry white wine

2 tablespoons hoisin sauce

2 tablespoons sherry

2 tablespoons honey

1 clove garlic, crushed

To Make Marinade: Mix together wine, hoisin, sherry, honey and garlic. Pour marinade over lamb and refrigerate for 2 hours.

Thread pieces of lamb and onions onto skewers. Grill or barbecue for 6 to 8 minutes and serve with a crisp salad.

SERVES 6

BALMAIN BUGS WITH LIME AND CORIANDER BUTTER

1 kg (2 lb) Balmain bugs

3 cloves garlic

2 tablespoons oil

LIME AND CORIANDER BUTTER

90 g (3 oz) butter

2 teaspoons grated lime rind

2 tablespoons lime juice

3 tablespoons chopped coriander

1 teaspoon cracked black pepper

To Make Lime and Coriander Butter: Place butter, lime rind and juice, coriander and pepper in a bowl and mix to combine.

Place butter down the centre of a piece of plastic wrap and roll into a log. Refrigerate until solid.

Place bugs, garlic and oil on a hot barbecue plate and toss for 3 to 4 minutes or until hot. Cut butter into rounds and serve with hot bugs.

SERVES 4 TO 6

BALMAIN BUGS

These are a species of crayfish and have an orange shell and white flesh. When purchased uncooked they are green, and cooked they are red. They should smell fresh. Keep cooked bugs in an airtight container in the refrigerator for up to 3 days, or freeze for 3 months. To get the most amount of meat, split bugs lengthwise.

Balmain Bugs with Lime and Coriander Butter

TANDOORI CHICKEN

16 chicken pieces, skinned

MARINADE

2 onions, grated

3 cloves garlic, crushed

4 tablespoons fresh lemon juice

TANDOORI PASTE

1½ cups (360 ml/12 fl oz) natural yoghurt

1 tablespoon ground coriander

2 teaspoons ground cumin

2 teaspoons turmeric

1 teaspoon ground chilli

red food colouring (optional)

Prick flesh of chicken with a fork.

To Make Marinade: Place onions, garlic and lemon juice in a bowl and mix to combine. Pour over chicken pieces and allow to stand for 30 minutes.

To Make Tandoori Paste: Place yoghurt, coriander, cumin, turmeric, chilli and food colouring in a bowl and mix to combine. Pour over chicken pieces and toss to evenly coat. Cover and refrigerate for 12 hours or overnight.

Cook chicken over glowing coals for 20 to 30 minutes or until cooked.

SERVES 8

Tandoori Chicken, Prawns with Creamy Satay Sauce

PRAWNS WITH CREAMY SATAY SAUCE

1 clove garlic, crushed

½ cup (125 g/4 oz) crunchy peanut butter

2 tablespoons soy sauce

2 tablespoons fresh lemon juice

2 teaspoons grated lemon rind

3 tablespoons water

1 red chilli, finely chopped

½ cup (125 ml/4 fl oz) cream

1 kg (2 lb) green prawns (shrimps), shelled and deveined with tails left intact

Place garlic, peanut butter, soy, lemon juice and rind, water and chilli in a small saucepan, stirring until sauce simmers and thickens. Stir through cream.

Thread prawns onto bamboo skewers and brush with satay sauce.

Cook prawns on barbecue or grill for 4 to 5 minutes basting with satay sauce.

Serve prawns hot with remaining satay sauce.

SERVES 8 TO 10

ITALIAN FISH PARCELS

2 x 1 kg (2 lb) whole fish, cleaned (whiting, bream, snapper)

⅓ cup (80 ml/2½ fl oz) fresh lemon juice

2 onions, sliced into rings

250 g (8 oz) mushrooms, sliced

4 tomatoes, sliced

pepper to taste

80 g (3 oz) butter

2 tablespoons lemon rind strips

Minted Lamb Burgers

Remove scales from fish and wash thoroughly. Place fish on separate pieces of foil.

Sprinkle fish with lemon juice, onion rings, mushrooms, tomatoes and pepper. Dot with butter and top with lemon rind strips. Seal fish in foil to make a package.

Barbecue over hot coals for 25 to 35 minutes. Serve fish with the vegetables and the juices in the foil.

SERVES 4 TO 6

MINTED LAMB BURGERS

MINTED BUTTER

    125 g (4 oz) butter, softened

    3 tablespoons chopped fresh mint

BURGERS

    1 kg (2 lb) lamb mince

    1 onion, finely chopped

    2 cloves garlic, crushed

    2 tablespoons chopped fresh mint

    1 teaspoon paprika

    1 egg, lightly beaten

To Make Minted Butter: Mix together butter and mint. Place on a sheet of plastic wrap and roll into a log shape. Chill until firm.

To Make Burgers: Place mince, onion, garlic, mint, paprika and egg in a bowl and mix well to combine.

Shape mixture into 6 patties. Cook over hot coals for 5 to 8 minutes or until cooked.

To serve place mint patties on bread rolls or buns and top with rounds of minted butter and salad of your choice.

SERVES 6

GLAZED SIRLOINS

6 sirloin steaks
(about 155 g/4½ oz each)

MARINADE

3 tablespoons soy sauce

3 tablespoons dry sherry

1 tablespoon Worcestershire sauce

2 cloves garlic, crushed

1 tablespoon white vinegar

2 tablespoons brown sugar

Trim steaks of any excess fat and place in a shallow container.

To Make Marinade: Place soy, sherry, Worcestershire, garlic, vinegar and sugar in a small bowl and mix to combine. Pour over steaks and refrigerate for 2 to 3 hours.

To cook, remove steaks from marinade and cook on a hot barbecue for 4 to 5 minutes each side. Brush with remaining marinade whilst cooking.

SERVES 6

RARE, MEDIUM OR WELL-DONE?

No two guests like their steak quite the same. How can you serve everyone hot food at the same time and be able to tell which steaks are rare and which are well done? Like so many things, it is easy once you know how. Cut your steaks to different thicknesses. Thick for rare, a little thinner for medium and so on. The bonus is that all are ready at the same time and you can easily tell, by the thickness, which is which. Serve more of the thinner ones of course!

BARBECUED FILLET WITH HORSERADISH CREAM

1½ kg (3 lb) fillet of beef

6 rashers bacon, rind removed

MARINADE

1 onion, roughly chopped

1 cup (250 ml/8 fl oz) port

4 peppercorns

1 clove garlic, crushed

HORSERADISH CREAM

1 cup (250 ml/8 fl oz) thickened cream, whipped

1 tablespoon horseradish cream

1 spring onion, finely sliced

1 tablespoon chopped fresh parsley

Remove any visible fat or sinew from meat. Wrap bacon around fillet in a spiral fashion and secure with toothpicks.

To Make Marinade: Place onion, port, peppercorns and garlic in a large plastic bag. Place fillet in bag and toss well to coat. Seal bag and refrigerate for 3 to 4 hours, turning bag occasionally. Remove fillet from marinade and barbecue until meat is cooked to your liking.

To Make Horseradish Cream: Fold together cream, horseradish, spring onion and parsley.

To serve, cut fillet into very thin slices and serve with horseradish cream.

SERVES 8

TIPS FOR BARBECUING SEAFOOD

Don't barbecue seafood over a flaming fire. Wait till the fire dies down to glowing embers. If using a metal plate this is not necessary, but grease the metal plate well. If using an electric barbecue, make sure the grill or plate is greased well.

Gas barbecuing is an ideal way to barbecue seafood as you have control over the temperature. Again, make sure the plate is greased.

Fish can be barbecued whole, filleted or as cutlets. Score larger fish — that is, cut through the flesh a few times to the bone on both sides, so that heat can penetrate.

LEMON AND PEPPER COD

Any fish cutlet can be used in this recipe.

6 cod cutlets

2 lemons, thinly sliced

2 tablespoons chopped fresh dill

2 tablespoons green peppercorns

½ cup (125 ml/4 fl oz) dry white wine

dill, to garnish

Place cod cutlets on 6 individual pieces of foil. Top each with lemon slices, dill and peppercorns.

Bring edges of foil together to form an open package. Drizzle a small amount of wine over each cutlet and seal foil edges together.

Barbecue packages for 8 to 10 minutes and serve with extra dill.

SERVES 6

Glazed Sirloins, Lemon and Pepper Cod

BARBECUED OREGANO CHICKEN

1 kg (2 lb) chicken pieces

2 teaspoons salt

MARINADE

½ cup (125 ml/4 fl oz) fresh lemon juice

1 tablespoon grated lemon rind

½ cup (125 ml/4 fl oz) olive oil

2 teaspoons cracked black pepper

4 tablespoons fresh oregano leaves, roughly chopped

Rub chicken pieces with salt, place in a bowl and allow to stand 5 minutes.

To Make Marinade: Mix together lemon juice, rind, oil, pepper and oregano. Pour over chicken pieces, cover with plastic wrap and refrigerate overnight.

Cook chicken pieces on barbecue basting frequently with marinade until cooked.

SERVES 4

CAJUN BLACKENED CHICKEN

6 chicken breast fillets

80 g (3 oz) butter, melted

CAJUN SPICE

2 cloves garlic, crushed

1 small onion, grated

1 tablespoon cracked black pepper

2 teaspoons chilli powder

1 tablespoon paprika

Brush both sides of chicken with butter.

To Make Cajun Spice: Mix together garlic, onion, pepper, chilli and paprika. Rub generously into chicken.

Barbecue on a smoking barbecue plate until outside of chicken is black and inside is tender.

SERVES 6

Barbecued Oregano Chicken

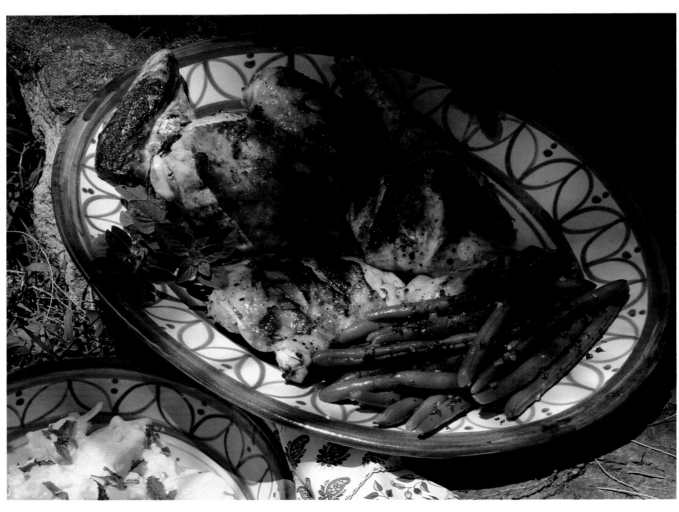

PEAR AND BLUE BRIE CHICKEN

6 chicken breast fillets

2 tablespoons lime juice

2 teaspoons sea salt

2 pears, peeled and chopped

60 g (2 oz) butter

200 g (7 oz) blue brie, sliced

Rub chicken with lime juice and salt. Place on a hot barbecue plate with pears and butter. Cook chicken and pears until golden brown on both sides.

Place brie slices over chicken and allow to melt slightly. Remove from barbecue and serve chicken with the golden pears.

SERVES 6

Pear and Blue Brie Chicken

RED MULLET
IN CORN HUSKS

6 small red mullet, cleaned and scaled

12 sprigs lemon thyme

1 lemon, sliced

2 cloves garlic, sliced

6 large corn husks

olive oil

cracked black pepper

Fill cavity of fish with thyme, lemon and garlic.

Place each fish on a corn husk. Drizzle with oil and pepper. Tie each end to the husks with string.

Place directly on coals or on barbecue and cook for 5 to 6 minutes or until fish is cooked.

SERVES 6

CHAR-GRILLED
SCALLOPS WITH
LIME HOLLANDAISE

500 g (1 lb) scallops

2 tablespoons olive oil

2 teaspoons cracked black pepper

LIME HOLLANDAISE

185 g (6 oz) butter

3 tablespoons water

3 egg yolks

1 tablespoon fresh lime juice

2 teaspoons lime rind

Thread scallops onto skewers. Drizzle with oil and sprinkle with pepper.

To Make Lime Hollandaise: Melt butter in a small saucepan and allow to cool. Place water and egg yolks in a bowl and whisk to combine. Place

bowl over a pan of simmering water and whisk until egg mixture is thick (about 3 minutes). Remove bowl from heat and slowly whisk in the butter. Stir through lime juice and rind.

Char-grill scallops on a hot barbecue, and serve, topped with Lime Hollandaise.

SERVES 4 TO 6

COOKING FISH

Fish fillets and cutlets are delicious barbecued. They can be cooked on the barbecue grill, or in foil over a medium to hot fire. If you are grilling over charcoal, damp the fire occasionally to replace lost moisture.

Don't overcook fish. It just becomes dried out and tasteless. Properly cooked fish is moist, tender and full of flavour. It is ready to eat when the flesh is just starting to flake.

Cooking time depends on thickness. Allow about 4 to 5 minutes a side for 2½ cm (1 in) thick fish cutlets. Turn carefully to cook other side. Brush with sauce or baste just before end of cooking time and serve hot. Marinating adds extra flavour to seafood. Popular marinade ingredients include lemon juice, white wine, oil, finely diced spring onions, soy or teriyaki sauces, fresh ginger and fresh herbs to taste. Marinades can also be used for basting during cooking.

Red Mullet in Corn Husks, Char-grilled Scallops with Lime Hollandaise

CHICKEN WITH SPICY PECAN STUFFING

4 chicken breast fillets

SPICY PECAN STUFFING

200 g (7 oz) cream cheese, softened

1 teaspoon ground cumin

1 teaspoon ground coriander

1 teaspoon ground chilli

¾ cup (90 g / 3 oz) chopped pecan nuts

Pound chicken until thin.

To Make Stuffing: Combine cream cheese, cumin, coriander, chilli and pecan nuts.

Place stuffing down the centre of each chicken fillet. Roll to enclose stuffing and secure with toothpicks.

Barbecue for 6 minutes or until tender. Slice and serve.

SERVES 4

BARBECUING POULTRY

Poultry has long been popular at barbecues with both cooks and guest. It's a flexible ingredient and a convenient finger food. Whole chickens can be spitroasted in 1 to 1½ hours, chicken pieces basted and barbecued and fillets from the breast or thigh cut into bite-sized chunks and served as kebabs or satés. Always buy good quality chicken, turkey or duck and same-sized pieces so that you can serve everyone hot food at the same time.

PIQUANT FISH STEAKS

4 fish steaks (tuna, salmon or halibut)

MARINADE

3 tablespoons fruity olive oil

10 fresh bay leaves, bruised

4 cardamon pods, bruised

2 teaspoons coriander seeds

2 tablespoons chopped chives

2 limes, sliced

2 teaspoons cracked black pepper

Place fish in a large shallow dish.

To Make Marinade: Place oil, bay leaves, cardamon, coriander, chives, lime and pepper in a small bowl and mix to combine. Pour marinade over fish. Cover and refrigerate for 3 to 4 hours, turning fish once.

Remove fish from marinade and barbecue until tender, brushing with marinade while cooking. Serve with a squeeze of lime or lemon.

SERVES 4

CHILLI BARBECUE PORK SPARE RIBS

1½ kg (3 lb) American pork spare ribs

MARINADE

1 cup (250 ml / 8 fl oz) tomato purée

2 tablespoons chilli sauce

2 tablespoons Worcestershire sauce

2 cloves garlic, crushed

2 tablespoons brown sugar

few drops Tabasco sauce

Trim ribs of any excess fat. Cut racks into single ribs. Place ribs in a large shallow dish.

To Make Marinade: Place tomato purée, chilli, Worcestershire, garlic, brown sugar and tabasco in a small bowl and mix to combine. Pour marinade over ribs, cover and refrigerate for 1 hour.

Cook ribs on a hot barbecue plate until tender, brushing with marinade while cooking.

SERVES 4 TO 6

SALT BAKED FISH

2 medium-sized fish (trout, sea bass or snapper), cleaned and scaled

4 sprigs dill

4 cloves garlic, halved

4 pieces lemon rind

10 peppercorns

salt

Fill cavity of fish with dill, garlic, lemon rind and peppercorns.

Lay 2 pieces of foil on a board and place a generous pile of salt down the middle of each piece of foil. Place fish on salt, cover with extra salt. Gather ends of foil and seal.

Place fish parcels on hot coals and cook for 15 to 20 minutes. Remove fish from foil and scrap away salt. Serve with salad.

SERVES 4 TO 6

WATCHING KILOJOULES

Barbecuing and spit-roasting meat are two of the least fattening ways of cooking meat. If you are watching your weight, buy lean cuts of meat and trim the fat off before cooking to reduce your cholesterol intake.

WARM SALAD OF BARBECUED BEEF AND RADICCHIO

500 g (1 lb) piece fillet steak

1 tablespoon oil

2 tablespoons light soy sauce

2 tablespoons fresh lemon juice

2 red chillies, seeded and chopped

2 cloves garlic, crushed

1 tablespoon shredded ginger

4 tablespoons red wine

2 heads radicchio, roughly torn into pieces

Slice fillet steak into thin pieces and place in a bowl with oil, soy, lemon juice, chilli, garlic, ginger and wine. Cover and refrigerate for 30 minutes.

Toss fillet steak, marinade and radicchio on a hot barbecue plate until tender. Serve warm.

SERVES 4

Warm Salad of Barbecued Beef and Radicchio

BEEF

Best quality beef is unsurpassed on its own or served with horseradish, mustards, savoury butters and sauces. Marinating also adds zest to a beef kebab or steak.

PORK AND NECTARINE ROLLS

4 pork schnitzels

NECTARINE FILLING

2 nectarines, seeded and sliced

1 cup (60 g/2 oz) fresh breadcrumbs

2 tablespoons honey

1 tablespoon chopped sage

4 spring onions, chopped

honey for glazing

Pound pork until thin.

To Make Filling: Combine nectarines, breadcrumbs, honey, sage and onions.

Place filling down the centre of the schnitzels. Roll pork over filling and tie with string.

Brush pork with extra honey and cook on barbecue for 10 minutes or until pork is tender. Slice and serve.

SERVES 4

BARBECUED PORK

Well done but not overdone is the rule for pork, so patience and care are required. Keep bastes and sauces free of fat because pork is such a rich meat. It goes well marinated in fruit flavours such as apricot or plum sauces and bastes. Buy the best pork. Ask your butcher for cuts without excess bone or fat. To cook crackling without overcooking the meat, take the rind off the meat and cook the skin separately. For crispy, crunchy crackling, rub the skin with oil and salt and cook over medium-to-hot coals.

CHILLI PEPPER YABBIES

12 uncooked yabbies or scampi

MARINADE

2 red chillies, seeded and chopped

½ cup (125 ml/4 fl oz) tomato purée

2 cloves garlic, crushed

6 spring onions, thinly sliced

2 tablespoons chopped fresh basil

3 teaspoons cracked black pepper

Make a small slit on the underside of each tail to allow marinade to soak through.

To Make Marinade: Place chilli, tomato, garlic, onions, basil and pepper in a large bowl and mix to combine. Add yabbies, cover and refrigerate for 1 hour.

Cook yabbies on a hot barbecue plate with marinade for 10 to 15 minutes or until flesh is tender. Serve with a leafy salad, and provide guests with nutcrackers.

SERVES 6

LOBSTER TAILS WITH MACADAMIAS

2 green lobster tails

MARINADE

3 tablespoons macadamia nut oil (or walnut oil)

2 tablespoons lemon thyme leaves

2 teaspoons grated lime rind

½ cup (30g/1 oz) chopped unsalted macadamia nuts

Cut lobster tails in half lengthwise.

To Make Marinade: Combine oil, thyme, rind and pepper in a small bowl.

Brush marinade over lobster flesh, cover and refrigerate for 1 hour.

Cook on barbecue flesh side down and brush with marinade until lobster is tender. Warm the macadamia nuts on the barbecue and serve on top of lobster.

SERVES 4

TANDOORI LAMB CUTLETS

12 lamb cutlets

MARINADE

1 cup (250 ml/8 fl oz) plain yoghurt

4 tablespoons chopped coriander leaves

1 tablespoon ground cumin

2 cloves garlic, crushed

1 tablespoon grated ginger

½ teaspoon turmeric

1 red chilli, seeded and finely chopped

Clean bones of cutlets and place in a large shallow dish.

To Make Marinade: Combine yoghurt, coriander, cumin, garlic, ginger, turmeric and chilli. Pour over cutlets, cover and refrigerate overnight.

Coat cutlets thickly in tandoori marinade and barbecue on a hot barbecue plate until tender. Serve with mint and salad.

SERVES 4

Lobster with Cress and Balsamic Vinegar

GOOD QUALITY MEAT

The golden rule is that good meat doesn't need to be tenderised. It is tender. Marinades offer extra flavours which broaden the barbecue repertoire in the same way as savoury butters and delicious sauces for dipping or pouring.

LOBSTER WITH CRESS AND BALSAMIC VINEGAR

2 green lobster tails

MARINADE

3 tablespoons balsamic vinegar

2 tablespoons brown sugar

2 tablespoons dry white wine

40 g (1½ oz) chopped watercress

1 tablespoon shredded lemon rind

Remove lobster flesh from shells and slice into thick medallions. Place in a shallow dish.

To Make Marinade: Place vinegar, sugar, wine, cress and lemon rind in a small bowl and mix to combine. Pour over lobster, cover and refrigerate for 30 minutes.

Barbecue lobster, brushing with marinade, until tender.

SERVES 4 TO 6

THAI CHICKEN WITH POTATO PANCAKES

6 chicken thigh fillets

4 tablespoons chopped coriander

2 stalks lemongrass, chopped

1 tablespoon chopped ginger

1 clove garlic, crushed

3 tablespoons sweet chilli sauce

POTATO PANCAKES

6 potatoes, grated

2 eggs, lightly beaten

3 tablespoons plain flour

2 tablespoons poppy seeds

Trim any excess fat from chicken and cut each thigh in half. Place in a shallow dish with coriander, lemongrass, ginger, garlic and chilli sauce. Cover and refrigerate for at least 2 hours.

Barbecue on a hot grill until tender.

To Make Potato Pancakes: Place potato, egg, flour and poppy seeds in a bowl and mix well to combine.

Cook heaped spoonfuls of mixture on a greased barbecue plate until golden brown on both sides.

To serve, place a small stack of pancakes on each plate and top with chicken pieces.

SERVES 6

CLEANING BARBECUES

A barbecue is much easier to clean when it is warm rather than when it is cold. Clean your barbecue after using it, or heat the barbecue plate before use and clean it.

PROSCIUTTO WRAPPED PORK FILLETS

4 small pork fillets

2 teaspoons dried marjoram

2 teaspoons freshly ground black pepper

2 cloves garlic, crushed

8 slices prosciutto

Trim any visible fat or sinew from fillets. Combine marjoram, pepper and garlic and roll fillets in this mixture.

Wrap prosciutto around fillets and secure with toothpicks. Cook on barbecue until tender. Serve sliced with fresh fruits.

SERVES 4 TO 6

VEAL WITH SWEET POTATO ROUNDS

6 veal steaks

MARINADE

½ cup (125 ml/4 fl oz) dry white wine

6 peppercorns

6 bay leaves

2 tablespoons chopped sage

1 large orange sweet potato, sliced

2 tablespoons honey

Place veal, wine, peppercorns, bay leaves and sage in a shallow dish and stand for 1 hour.

Brush both sides of potato slices with honey.

Place sweet potato rounds on a well-greased barbecue. Place veal on barbecue and brush with marinade. Cook until veal and potatoes are tender.

SERVES 6

CRISPY PRAWNS WITH MANGO SALSA

These prawns can be eaten with their crispy shells or peeled.

1 kg (2 lb) green prawns (shrimps)

2 cloves garlic, crushed

2 tablespoons shredded lemon rind

2 red chillies, seeded and chopped

2 teaspoons ground cumin

2 tablespoons olive oil

2 tablespoons chopped fresh coriander

MANGO SALSA

1 mango, peeled and chopped

2 tablespoons chopped fresh mint

1 teaspoon cracked black pepper

2 teaspoons honey

Place prawns, garlic, lemon rind, chilli, cumin, oil and coriander in a bowl and toss to combine. Cover and stand for 1 hour.

Place prawns in their shells and marinade on a hot barbecue plate and cook until crisp.

To Make Salsa: Place mango, mint, pepper and honey in a bowl and mix to combine. Refrigerate until required.

Serve prawns with mango salsa.

SERVES 6

Crispy Prawns with Mango Salsa, Thai Chicken with Potato Pancakes

SPICY BARBECUED LAMB LEG

1 leg lamb, boned and butterflied

MARINADE

  4 tablespoons chopped fresh coriander

  1 tablespoon black mustard seeds

  3 tablespoons fresh lemon juice

  3 tablespoons sweet soy sauce

  3 tablespoons sweet chilli sauce

Trim excess fat and sinew from lamb. Place lamb in a large shallow dish.

To Make Marinade: Combine coriander, mustard seeds, lemon juice, soy and chilli sauce. Rub over lamb. Cover and refrigerate overnight.

Barbecue until lamb is tender. Brush frequently while cooking. Serve sliced with flat-bread and salad.

SERVES 6 TO 8

SALMON WITH COCONUT CORIANDER SALSA

  6 salmon cutlets

  60 g (2 oz) butter

  3 tablespoons fresh lemon juice

COCONUT CORIANDER SALSA

  1 cup (90 g/3 oz) desiccated coconut

  3 tablespoons water

  2 green chillies, seeded and chopped

  2 teaspoons oil

  1 teaspoon black mustard seeds

  3 tablespoons chopped fresh coriander

Wash and dry salmon. Place butter and lemon juice on a hot barbecue plate and heat until foaming. Cook salmon until tender.

To Make Salsa: Place coconut, water and chilli in a food processor or blender and process until smooth. Heat oil in a small pan, add mustard seeds and cook until they pop.

Add coconut mixture and cook for a further 3 minutes. Stir through coriander. Serve salmon with warm or cold salsa.

SERVES 6

MOROCCAN LAMB FILLETS

  6 lamb fillets

  2 tablespoons tomato paste

  2 teaspoons ground cinnamon

  1 red onion, finely grated

  3 tablespoons chopped fresh parsley

  2 red chillies, seeded and chopped

Trim fillets of any fat or sinew. Place in a large shallow dish with tomato paste, cinnamon, onion, parsley and chilli. Cover and stand for at least 2 hours.

Barbecue on a hot grill until tender. Serve with a citrus-based salad and bread.

SERVES 6

CONTROL THE HEAT

Flame does not cook meat, it burns fat. Control the heat by damping charcoal, or by moving food to one side with gas. When damping, sprinkle water carefully, just to reduce the temperature. Don't overdo it. If your grill is very close to the coals, move food to one side while you damp down.

Salmon with Coconut Coriander Salsa

Seafood Selection

1 *Blue swimmer crab* 2 *Lobster*
3 *Barramundi* 4 *Yabbies*
5 *Balmain bugs* 6 *Red mullet* 7 *Garfish*
8 *Green-lipped mussels* 9 *Snapper*
10 *Baby octopus* 11 *Prawns* 12 *Scallops*
13 *Sardines*

Breads and Spreads

A selection of interesting and tasty breads transforms a barbecue into something special. Filled breads can almost form a meal in themselves! Prepare them before the guests arrive and then bake them in the coals or bake them in the oven so that you have something to serve immediately. The spreads below will transform the plainest bread into a treat.

SAVOURY BUTTERS

Savoury butters with herbs and spices can be made in advance and stored in the refrigerator. Mix together butter and herbs, roll in greaseproof paper into a log shape, then wrap tightly in freezer paper and foil. Store in the freezer and slice pats as required. Savoury butters are great with sizzling steaks and vegetables. Try some of these suggestions:

• Cream butter with finely mashed anchovy fillets. Use with fish and veal.
• Pound fresh basil in a mortar and pestle and cream into butter. Delicious with vegetables, rice or pasta.
• Beat butter with French mustard and horseradish. Excellent with meat or fish.
• Cream butter with either fresh dill, fresh garlic with parsley, fresh chives and parsley, freshly ground black pepper or fresh rosemary. Use whatever you favour and invent your own combinations.

Flat Bread with Sesame Topping, Salmon and Dill Butter, Pecorino and Herb Butter, Mustard Pepperoni Butter

FLAT BREAD WITH SESAME TOPPING

90 g (3 oz) butter, softened

2 tablespoons mixed dried herbs

8 flat bread rounds, cut into large wedges

3 tablespoons sesame seeds

Preheat oven to 180°C (350°F).

Melt butter in a small saucepan and stir through herbs.

Brush butter mixture over flat breads. Place on an oven slide and sprinkle with sesame seeds.

Bake for 15 minutes or until crisp.

SERVES 8

MUSTARD PEPPERONI BUTTER

125 g (4 oz) butter, softened

⅓ cup (80 g/3 oz) pepperoni, finely chopped

1 tablespoon mustard

1 tablespoon chopped chives

Place butter in a small bowl and beat until light and smooth.

Stir through pepperoni, mustard and chives. Serve with barbecued vegetables and meats.

SALMON AND DILL BUTTER

125 g (4 oz) butter, softened

60 g (2 oz) smoked salmon trimmings, chopped

2 to 3 tablespoons chopped fresh dill

2 teaspoons cracked black pepper

Place butter in a bowl and beat until light and smooth.

Stir through salmon, dill and pepper. Refrigerate until needed. Serve with bread or on barbecued vegetables or meats.

PECORINO AND HERB BUTTER

125 g (4 oz) butter, softened

¼ cup (30 g/1 oz) grated pecorino cheese

3 tablespoons chopped fresh mixed herbs

2 teaspoons cracked black pepper

Place butter in a small bowl and beat until light and smooth.

Stir through cheese, herbs and pepper. Refrigerate until required. Serve with barbecued vegetables or meats.

CHILLI BUTTER

125 g (4 oz) butter, softened

1 to 2 teaspoons ground chilli

few drops Tabasco sauce

1 tablespoon tomato paste

Place butter in a small bowl and beat until light and smooth.

Stir through chilli, Tabasco and tomato paste. Great served with hamburgers and meats.

FRUIT AND TEA DAMPER

½ cup (60 g) chopped dried apricots

½ cup (90 g) chopped raisins

¾ cup (125 g) dried dates, pitted and chopped

finely grated rind 1 orange

2 cups (500 ml/16 fl oz) warm tea

60 g (2 oz) butter, softened

1 teaspoon allspice

2 tablespoons sugar

1 quantity Damper dough (see below)

Combine fruits in a small bowl, cover with tea and set aside for 30 minutes to soak. Drain very well then combine with butter, allspice and sugar.

Pat damper dough out to form a circle approximately 30 cm (12 in) in diameter. Place fruit in the centre. Fold edges of circle towards centre (the circle should now be a square) and pinch edges together to encase filling.

Carefully place fruit damper on a greased baking tray and brush lightly with a little beaten egg. Bake at 200°C (400°F) for 25 minutes, then reduce heat to 180°C (350°F) and bake a further 15 to 20 minutes, or until well risen.

Cool slightly before serving, otherwise the filling will be too hot.

SERVES 8

DAMPER

4 cups (500 g/1 lb) self-raising flour

1 teaspoon salt

30 g (1 oz) butter

1 cup (250 ml/8 fl oz) milk

½ cup (125 ml/4 fl oz) water

Preheat oven to 200°C (400°F).

Sift flour and salt into a large bowl. Rub butter through flour with fingertips.

Damper, Fruit and Tea Damper

Make a well in the centre of the flour and add milk and water. Mix with a knife until mixture forms a soft dough.

Place on a floured board and knead until smooth. Form dough into a large round.

Place on a greased and floured oven tray and bake for 25 to 35 minutes or until cooked.

SERVES 8

HAM AND BLUE CHEESE BREAD

1 loaf of bread of your choice

FILLING

- *100 g (3½ oz) butter, softened*
- *60 g (2 oz) ham, finely sliced*
- *60 g (2 oz) creamy blue vein cheese*
- *2 tablespoons chopped fresh parsley*
- *2 teaspoons cracked black pepper*

Preheat oven to 200°C (400°F).

Cut bread loaf into thick slices.

To Make Filling: Place butter, ham, cheese, parsley and pepper in a small bowl and mix to combine.

Spread bread slices with filling and put loaf back together. Wrap in foil and bake for 10 minutes.

Open top of foil and bake for a further 10 minutes or until loaf is crisp.

SERVES 6 TO 8

BARBECUE BREADS

Just about any bread goes with a barbecue. French bread sticks are hard to beat and so are wholegrain bread rolls, rye, black bread, plaits, herb breads and sour dough. Few people have time to make bread these days and there is really no need as there are some excellent breads to buy. You can transform the average bread loaf into something special with herbed and savoury butters.
For special occasions make damper or buttermilk bread — so easy and you will make a great impression. Add a handful of your favourite herbs to the mixture for something different.

CHEESE AND CHIVE BREAD

1 loaf of bread of your choice

FILLING

- *60 g (2 oz) butter, softened*
- *150 g (5 oz) cream cheese*
- *1 cup (125 g/4 oz) grated cheddar cheese*
- *2 tablespoons chopped fresh parsley*
- *4 tablespoons chopped fresh chives*
- *1 teaspoon cracked black pepper*

Preheat oven to 200°C (400°F).

Cut bread loaf into thick slices.

To Make Filling: Place butter, cheeses, parsley, chives and pepper in a small bowl and mix to combine.

Spread bread slices with filling and put loaf back together. Wrap in foil and bake for 10 minutes.

Open top of foil and bake for a further 10 minutes or until loaf is crisp and cheese has melted.

SERVES 6 TO 8

GARLIC AND HERB BREAD

1 loaf of bread of your choice

FILLING

- *100 g (3½ oz) butter, softened*
- *3 cloves garlic, crushed*
- *20 g (¾ oz) chopped fresh mixed herbs*
- *1 tablespoon Worcestershire sauce*
- *2 teaspoons cracked black pepper*
- *1 cup (125 g/4 oz) grated cheddar cheese*

Preheat oven to 200°C (400°F).

Cut bread into slices but do not cut all the way through.

To Make Filling: Place butter, garlic, herbs, Worcestershire and pepper in a bowl and mix to combine.

Spread bread slices with filling and wrap loaf in foil. Bake for 10 minutes.

Open top of foil and sprinkle loaf with cheese. Return to oven for 10 minutes or until cheese melts.

SERVES 6 TO 8

BUTTERMILK BREAD

- *2 cups (250 g/8 oz) wholemeal flour*
- *2¼ cups (280 g/9 oz) plain flour*
- *1 teaspoon salt*
- *2 teaspoons bicarbonate of soda*
- *1¼ cups (300 ml/10 fl oz) buttermilk*

Preheat oven to 220°C (450°F).

Sift flours, salt and bicarbonate of soda and stir in buttermilk a little at a time. Beat until dough is firm and leaves sides of bowl clean. Turn onto floured surface and knead until smooth.

Shape into flattish round loaf 20 cm (8 in) in diameter. Place on a greased baking tray and, using a sharp knife, cut a deep cross in the top. Bake for 25 to 30 minutes.

SERVES 4

PATAFLA

1 baguette or long French stick

FILLING

6 tomatoes, peeled and chopped

6 spring onions, finely chopped

2 green capsicums (peppers), chopped

1 red capsicum (pepper), chopped

200 g (7 oz) black olives, pitted and chopped

1 tablespoon capers, chopped

4 gherkins, chopped

2 teaspoons cracked black pepper

1 tablespoon grain mustard

Cut bread in half lengthways. Scoop out most of the soft bread.

To Make Filling: Place tomatoes, spring onions, capsicums, olives, capers, gherkins, pepper and mustard in a small bowl and mix to combine.

Spoon filling into hollowed bread. Press both halves together, wrap in foil and refrigerate for 1 hour. To serve cut into slices.

SERVES 10

FRENCH ONION LOAF

1 loaf of bread of your choice

FILLING

250 g (8 oz) cream cheese

1 packet French onion soup mix

Preheat oven to 200°C (400°F).

Cut bread loaf into thick slices.

To Make Filling: Combine cream cheese and soup mix in a bowl.

Clockwise from bottom left: French Onion Loaf, Patafla, Cheese and Bacon Loaf

Spread bread slices with filling and put loaf back together. Wrap in foil and bake for 10 minutes.

Open top of foil and bake for a further 10 minutes or until loaf is crisp.

SERVES 6 TO 8

CHEESE AND BACON LOAF

3 cups (375 g/12 oz) self-raising flour

1 teaspoon salt

60 g (2 oz) butter

1 cup (250 ml/8 fl oz) milk

FILLING

2 rashers bacon, chopped and cooked

1 cup (125 g/4 oz) grated cheddar cheese

1 tablespoon grain mustard

½ teaspoon paprika

1 egg, lightly beaten

Preheat oven to 200°C (400°F).

Sift flour and salt into a large bowl. Rub butter through flour with fingertips.

Make a well in the centre and add milk. Mix with a knife to form a smooth dough. Knead lightly on a well-floured board. Roll out dough to form a 30 x 25 cm (12 x 10 in) rectangle.

To Make Filling: Combine bacon, cheese, mustard and paprika. Spread filling over dough and roll dough, starting at the longest edge, to form a rolled loaf.

Place loaf on a greased oven tray, brush with egg and bake for 20 to 30 minutes.

SERVES 6

In the Shade of the Garden

*O*n a hot summer's day, sit back and relax under the shade of a tree and treat yourself and your guests to these delicious dishes, that are so easy to make. Have lunch or afternoon tea in the garden in gourmet style.

SMOKED CHICKEN FOCACCIA

4 squares focaccia, split in half

4 smoked chicken breast fillets

125 g (4 oz) sun-dried capsicum (pepper), sliced

2 peaches, sliced

8 curly lettuce leaves

3 tablespoons mayonnaise

Fill focaccia with chicken, capsicums and peaches. Toast until warm. Fill with lettuce and mayonnaise and serve.

SERVES 4

ASPARAGUS AND GORGONZOLA SLICE

2 bunches asparagus

3 tablespoons chopped chives

125 g (4 oz) gorgonzola cheese, crumbled

1 cup (125 g/4 oz) self-raising flour

60 g (2 oz) butter, melted

5 eggs

1 cup (250 ml/8 fl oz) milk

1 teaspoon cracked black pepper

Preheat oven to 180°C (350°F).

Lightly steam asparagus until tender. Place chives, gorgonzola, flour, butter, eggs, milk and pepper in a bowl and mix to combine.

Place asparagus in a greased 16 x 26 cm (6 x 10 in) tin. Pour over egg mixture and bake for 30 to 40 minutes or until set and golden brown. Serve warm or cold.

SERVES 6

Picture previous pages: Ratatouille Tart, Warm Summer Pasta, Smoked Salmon Sandwiches (recipes page 55)

Below: Asparagus and Gorgonzola Slice

SMOKED SALMON SANDWICHES

8 large slices smoked salmon

125 g (4 oz) watercress, tips only

8 slices bread or 4 bread rolls

LIME MAYONNAISE

½ cup (125 ml/4 fl oz) mayonnaise

1 tablespoon fresh lime juice

2 teaspoons lime rind

1 teaspoon cracked black pepper

Arrange smoked salmon and watercress on bread.

To Make Lime Mayonnaise: Mix together mayonnaise, lime juice and rind and pepper.

Spoon mayonnaise over salmon and retreat to a quiet corner of the garden to eat.

SERVES 4

RATATOUILLE TART

PASTRY

125 g (4 oz) butter, chopped

250 g (8 oz) plain flour

1 egg

1 to 2 tablespoons water

RATATOUILLE

2 eggplants (aubergines), diced

salt

2 red onions, chopped

1 tablespoon olive oil

2 cloves garlic, crushed

2 green capsicums (peppers), chopped

4 zucchini (courgettes), chopped

5 tomatoes, peeled, seeded and chopped

2 tablespoon chopped fresh basil

2 tablespoons chopped fresh oregano

cracked black pepper

1 cup (125 g/4 oz) grated mature cheddar

To Make Pastry: Place butter and flour in a food processor and process until mixture resembles fine crumbs. Add the egg and enough water to form a soft dough. Knead pastry lightly, cover with plastic wrap and refrigerate for 30 minutes.

Preheat oven to 180°C (350°F). Roll pastry to fit a 30 cm (12 in) tart tin. Prick base and sides and bake for 15 minutes or until crisp and golden.

To Prepare Ratatouille: Place eggplant in a colander and sprinkle with salt. Allow to drain for 20 minutes. Wash and dry. Sauté onions in oil until golden brown.

Add garlic, capsicums, zucchini, tomatoes, eggplant, herbs, and pepper to taste. Simmer for 30 to 40 minutes. Cool slightly.

Place in tart shell. Sprinkle with cheese and return to oven for 12 minutes or until cheese melts. Serve warm or cold.

SERVES 6 TO 8

WARM SUMMER PASTA

5 tomatoes, peeled and chopped

8 sun-dried tomatoes, sliced

60 g (2 oz) pitted black olives, chopped

3 tablespoons shredded basil

2 tablespoons balsamic vinegar

500 g (1 lb) ribbon type pasta

1 tablespoon olive oil

2 cloves garlic, crushed

2 tablespoons chopped fresh sage

6 slices spicy salami, cut into strips

grated Parmesan cheese, to serve

Place tomatoes, olives, basil and vinegar in a bowl and stand for 30 minutes.

Cook pasta in boiling water until tender, drain and keep warm.

Heat oil in a large pan and sauté garlic, sage and salami until golden. Remove from heat and toss through pasta and tomato mixture. Serve warm with Parmesan cheese and bread.

SERVES 4 TO 6

MUSHROOM AND ROASTED PEPPER RISOTTO

3 tablespoons butter

2 cloves garlic, crushed

1 onion, finely chopped

250 g (8 oz) button mushrooms, halved

440 g (14 oz) arborio rice

10 cups (2½ litres/80 fl oz) hot chicken or vegetable stock

1 red capsicum (pepper), halved

1 green capsicum (pepper), halved

2 tablespoons chopped chives

cracked black pepper

Heat butter in a large pan. Add garlic and onion and sauté until brown. Add mushrooms and cook for 1 minute.

Add rice to pan and cook for 2 minutes. Add 2 cups (500 ml/16 fl oz) of stock to pan at a time stirring constantly until stock is absorbed.

Grill capsicums skin side up until charred and soft. Peel away skins and chop. Stir through risotto with chives and pepper, and serve.

SERVES 6

COCONUT ROUGH COOKIES

2 egg whites

1½ cups (70 g/2½ oz) shredded coconut

⅔ cup (125 g/4 oz) icing sugar

1 teaspoon vanilla essence

½ cup (90 g/3 oz) grated white chocolate

Preheat oven to 200°C (400°F).

Place egg whites in a bowl with coconut, icing sugar, vanilla and chocolate. Mix well to form a stiff paste.

Place spoonfuls of mixture on baking trays and bake for 12 to 15 minutes or until light golden brown. Serve with scented tea.

MAKES 20

TANGELO SYRUP CAKE

250 g (8 oz) butter

2 tablespoons grated tangelo rind

1 cup (220 g/7 oz) caster sugar

3 eggs, separated

2 cups (250 g/8 oz) self-raising flour, sifted

½ cup (125 ml/4 fl oz) buttermilk

½ cup (125 ml/4 fl oz) yoghurt

1 teaspoon vanilla essence

TANGELO SYRUP

4 tablespoons tangelo juice

¾ cup (185 g/6 oz) sugar

3 tablespoons water

Preheat oven to 180°C (375°F).

Beat together butter, rind and sugar until light and creamy. Add egg yolks and beat well. Fold through flour, buttermilk, yoghurt and vanilla.

Beat egg whites until stiff and fold through mixture. Pour into a greased 20 cm (8 in) round cake tin and bake for 1 hour or until cooked.

To Make Tangelo Syrup: Place juice, sugar and water in a small pan and stir over low heat until sugar dissolves. Simmer syrup for 3 minutes.

Pour hot syrup over hot, turned-out cake. Serve warm with cream.

SERVES 8

BABY LEMON MERINGUE PIES

LEMON FILLING

125 g (4 oz) butter

1 cup (250 g/8 oz) sugar

2 eggs, lightly beaten

½ cup (125 ml/4 fl oz) fresh lemon juice

12 small ready-made pastry shells

MERINGUE TOPPING

3 egg whites

¾ cup (185 g/6 oz) caster sugar

To Make Lemon Filling: Place butter, sugar, eggs and lemon juice in the top of a double boiler. Stir over low heat until mixture is thick. Cool and place in pie shells.

To Make Meringue: Beat egg whites until stiff. Gradually add sugar, beating well. Top pies with a generous spoonful of meringue. Place until a medium grill and cook until lightly browned.

MAKES 12

Baby Lemon Meringue Pies, Tangelo Syrup Cake

Portable Picnics

A picnic is often a spur-of-the-moment meal, thrown together from staples found in the pantry, so the family can take advantage of an unexpectedly fine day. But with a small amount of forethought and planning, a picnic can become a treat, with any setting you choose. Spread out the blanket, or take the table and chairs, add some sparkling wine or fruit juice, and the picnic turns into an outdoor feast.

Basket and rug from Country Road, plates from Accoutrement, glass from Orrefors Kosta Boda

SESAME CHEESE PIE

500 g (1 lb) ricotta cheese

1¼ cups (300 ml/10 fl oz) sour cream

2 eggs, lightly beaten

1 cup (125 g/4 oz) grated cheddar cheese

4 spring onions, chopped

2 tablespoons chopped fresh mint

1 bunch chives, chopped

375 g (12 oz) puff pastry

1 egg, lightly beaten, extra

2 tablespoons sesame seeds

Preheat oven to 190°C (375°F).

Place ricotta, sour cream, eggs, cheese, onions, mint and chives in a bowl and mix well to combine.

Roll half of the puff pastry to form a rectangle 18 x 33 cm (7 x 13 in). Place pastry on a baking tray. Spoon over filling leaving a 3 cm (1 in) border. Roll remaining half of pastry to fit over filling. Brush edges with extra egg and press edges together.

Make a few cuts in the top of the pastry to allow steam to escape. Brush with egg and sprinkle with sesame seeds. Bake for 25 to 35 minutes or until golden brown. Serve warm or cold cut into wedges.

SERVES 6

STACKED PICNIC LOAF

1 Vienna loaf

HAM FILLING

8 slices double smoked ham

3 tablespoons pickles

1 small cucumber, sliced

1 red capsicum (pepper), sliced

CHEESE FILLING

8 slices Swiss cheese

2 tomatoes, sliced

1 curly lettuce, shredded

1 carrot, grated

Cut 8 slices in the loaf but not all the way through. Place a piece of ham in the first bread slice. Spread with pickles and stack with cucumber and capsicum.

Fill the next bread slice with cheese, tomato, lettuce and carrot. Repeat fillings alternately.

Wrap loaf in paper and plastic wrap. Unwrap loaf at your picnic destination and cut the required sandwich stack from the loaf.

SERVES 4 TO 6

POTATO AND BACON SALAD

3 rashers bacon, chopped

1¼ kg (2½ lb) baby new potatoes, peeled

3 tablespoons good quality salad dressing

1 cup (250 ml/8 fl oz) mayonnaise

2 tablespoons chopped fresh chives

1 teaspoon cracked black pepper

Sauté bacon until crisp. Drain on absorbent paper and allow to cool. Cut potatoes in half and boil until tender. Drain and refresh with cold water.

Place salad dressing, mayonnaise, chives and pepper in a bowl and mix to combine. Pour over potatoes, add bacon, toss and chill until ready to serve.

SERVES 6

SPINACH TORTILLA

Tortillas are Spanish-style omelettes and make great, easily transportable picnic food.

1 tablespoon olive oil

1 red onion, chopped

2 potatoes, chopped

8 spinach leaves, shredded

200 ml (6½ fl oz) light sour cream

6 eggs, lightly beaten

1 teaspoon cracked black pepper

2 tablespoons chopped fresh parsley

Heat oil in a large, non-stick fry pan. Add onion and potatoes and sauté over low heat until soft. Add spinach leaves and cook until wilted.

Mix together sour cream, eggs, pepper and parsley and pour into pan. Cook over low heat until almost set. Place under a hot grill to brown the top.

Allow to cool in pan. Turn tortilla out of pan and serve cut into wedges with crusty bread.

SERVES 6

SAND-WEDGES

1 round rye bread

FILLING

4 tablespoons ready-made pesto

12 slices spicy salami

4 tomatoes, sliced

12 thick slices camembert

12 English spinach leaves

Picture previous pages: Stacked Picnic Loaf (page 60), Spinach Tortilla (page 60), Peach and Raspberry Tarts (page 67)

Pork and Veal Terrine, Potato and Bacon Salad

1 yellow capsicum (pepper), sliced

1 cucumber, thinly sliced

Cut top from bread round. Scoop out soft bread filling, leaving a 2 cm (1 in) wall. Spread inside of bread with pesto.

Layer half the salami, tomatoes, camembert, spinach, capsicum and cucumber. Repeat these layers. Replace the top and tie securely with string. Cut into wedges to serve.

SERVES 6

PORK AND VEAL TERRINE

1 onion, finely chopped

1 clove garlic, crushed

1 teaspoon butter

1 kg (2 lb) pork and veal mince

250 g (8 oz) chicken livers, minced

2 eggs, lightly beaten

1 tablespoon chopped fresh sage

1 teaspoon fresh thyme

3 tablespoons brandy

1 teaspoon cracked black pepper

8 rashers bacon

Preheat oven to 180°C (350°F).

Sauté onion and garlic in butter until soft. Place in a large bowl with mince, livers, eggs, sage, thyme, brandy and pepper and mix well to combine.

Line a terrine dish with overlapping slices of bacon. Press mixture into terrine and fold overlapping bacon slices over mixture to seal. Cover with foil and place terrine in a deep baking dish. Add enough water to come halfway up the sides of the terrine.

Bake for 1½ hours. Drain any excess liquid from terrine and refrigerate until cold. Serve sliced with crusty bread.

SERVES 8

PRAWN AND CHEESE TARTS

PASTRY

1½ cups (185g/6 oz) plain flour

100 g (3½ oz) butter

½ cup (60 g/2 oz) grated cheddar cheese

2 tablespoons cold water

FILLING

½ cup (185 g/6 oz) chopped cooked prawns (shrimps)

1 cup (125 g/4 oz) grated tasty cheese

2 spring onions, chopped

4 eggs, lightly beaten

½ cup (125 ml/4 fl oz) cream

½ cup (125 ml/4 fl oz) milk

2 teaspoons grated lemon rind

1 teaspoon cracked black pepper

Preheat oven to 190°C (375°F).

Place flour and butter in a food processor and process until mixture resembles fine breadcrumbs. Add cheese and enough water to form a smooth dough.

Knead pastry lightly on a floured board. Roll out dough thinly and cut 24 x 6 cm (2½ in) rounds of dough. Press pastry into patty tins.

Top with a small spoonful of prawns. Place cheese, onions, eggs, cream, milk, rind and pepper in a small bowl and mix to combine.

Pour egg mixture into pastry cases and bake for 15 to 20 minutes or until puffed and golden. Serve warm or cold.

SERVES 6 TO 8

POCKET PASTRIES

375 g (12 oz) packet filo pastry

200 g (7 oz) butter, melted

SEAFOOD FILLING

¼ cup (60 g/2 oz) cottage cheese

250 g (8 oz) canned crab meat, drained

2 spring onions, chopped

1 teaspoon cracked black pepper

CHEESE AND SPINACH FILLING

6 spinach leaves, shredded and cooked

1 small onion, chopped

60 g (2 oz) fetta cheese

½ teaspoon fresh lemon juice

½ teaspoon cracked black pepper

CHILLI MEAT FILLING

125 g (4 oz) cooked minced meat

1 tablespoon chilli sauce

1 tablespoon tomato paste

1 small onion, chopped

CREAM CHEESE FILLING

125 g (4 oz) cream cheese, softened

2 spring onions, chopped

2 teaspoons wholegrain mustard

½ teaspoon cracked black pepper

Preheat oven to 200°C (400°F).

To Prepare the Separate Fillings: Combine relevant ingredients in a bowl and mix to combine.

Take 2 sheets of pastry and place one on top of the other. Cut pastry in 6 pieces across the width. Brush each piece with a little butter.

Place a spoonful of the selected filling in left corner of pastry. Fold other corner of pastry over to form a triangle shape. Keep folding in a triangle form until the end of pastry. Brush pastry triangles with butter.

Repeat with remaining sheets of pastry and fillings.

Bake for 15 to 20 minutes or until golden.

MAKES ABOUT 50

FILO PASTRY

If you are using frozen filo pastry, make sure you thaw it first. Frozen pastry is brittle and breaks easily. Leave it unopened at room temperature for about 3 hours before using. If you are using chilled filo, leave it at room temperature for 1 to 2 hours.

While you are preparing the filling, cover the pastry with a dry cloth then a moist one to prevent the pastry drying out. Don't let the pastry come into direct contact with the wet cloth as the sheets will stick together.

Brush pastry sheets with butter for a rich flavour, especially if you are making a dessert. But if you are watching your cholesterol intake, use olive oil. This is best used on savoury pastries.

Prawn and Cheese Tarts, Pocket Pastries

SAGE AND ONION ROLLS

2 teaspoons olive oil

1 onion, finely chopped

500 g (1 lb) minced beef

3 tablespoons chopped fresh sage

2 tablespoons chopped fresh parsley

1 teaspoon cracked black pepper

250 g (8 oz) shortcrust pastry

1 egg, lightly beaten

Preheat oven to 190°C (375°F).

Heat oil in a small fry pan and sauté onion until soft. Place in a bowl with mince, sage, parsley and pepper and mix well to combine.

Cut prepared pastry in half. Roll each piece into a 36 x 12 cm (14 x 5 in) rectangle. Pile mixture down the centre of each pastry piece.

Brush edges with beaten egg and bring pastry over filling and overlap slightly to form a roll. Cut each roll into 6 individual rolls and brush with egg.

Place rolls on a baking tray and bake for 15 minutes or until golden and cooked. Serve warm or cold.

SERVES 6

ITALIAN BEEF ROULADE

2 x 500 g (1 lb) pieces rump steak

FILLING

6 slices prosciutto

8 sun-dried tomatoes, chopped

60 g (2 oz) pitted black olives, chopped

2 tablespoons shredded basil

6 artichoke hearts, finely chopped

2 cups (125 g/4 oz) fresh breadcrumbs

1 tablespoon green peppercorns

Preheat oven to 200°C (400°F).

Trim fat from steaks. Pound until 1 cm (1/2 in) thick. Overlap pieces of steak to form one large piece. Lay prosciutto over steaks.

To Prepare Filling: Place tomatoes, olives, basil, artichokes, breadcrumbs and peppercorns in a bowl and mix to combine.

Place filling down the centre and roll meat around to form a tight parcel. Tie with string and place on a baking tray. Bake for 1 hour or until cooked through. Allow to cool. Slice and serve.

SERVES 6 TO 8

SUN-DRIED TOMATOES

Sun-dried tomatoes can be purchased in the dried form or marinated in oil, often with garlic, herbs or spices. They have a very concentrated flavour and a dark red colour. If you buy them unmarinated, soak them in warm water for at least 30 minutes before using.

Italian Beef Roulade

CHOCOLATE NUT SLICE

- *125 g (4 oz) butter*
- *½ cup (90 g/3 oz) brown sugar*
- *1 tablespoon golden syrup*
- *2 tablespoons cocoa*
- *1 egg, beaten*
- *½ teaspoon vanilla*
- *250 g (8 oz) plain sweet biscuits, crushed*
- *½ cup (60 g/2 oz) chopped nuts (walnuts, almonds or pecans)*
- *2 tablespoons desiccated coconut*

ICING

- *90 g (3 oz) chocolate*
- *3 tablespoons water*
- *1 teaspoon oil*
- *2 cups (370 g/12 oz) icing sugar, sifted*
- *¼ cup (30 g/1 oz) finely chopped nuts (walnuts, almonds or pecans)*

Combine butter, sugar, golden syrup and cocoa in saucepan. Stir over low heat to dissolve sugar, then heat until bubbling.

Remove from heat and add beaten egg and vanilla, stirring until thick. Add crushed biscuits, nuts and coconut and mix well. Press mixture into greased 28 x 18 cm lamington tin. Chill until firm.

To Make Icing: Combine chocolate, water and oil in a bowl. Place over hot water to melt. Add icing sugar and stir well to combine. Spread chocolate icing over slice. Sprinkle with nuts. Allow icing to set before cutting into squares or fingers to serve.

MAKES ABOUT 20

FRUIT STRUDEL JAFFLES

Try different types of canned fruit instead of apple.

- *500 g (1 lb) canned pie apples*
- *¾ cup (125 g/4 oz) sultanas*
- *3 tablespoons chopped raisins*
- *1 tablespoon grated lemon rind*
- *½ cup (60 g/2 oz) chopped walnuts*
- *1 tablespoon mixed spice*
- *2 tablespoons sugar*
- *900 g (1 lb 13 oz) ready-rolled shortcrust pastry*
- *45 g (1½ oz) butter, melted*

Combine apple, sultanas, raisins, rind, walnuts, spice and sugar in a bowl and mix well.

Cut pastry sheets according to size of electric sandwich maker. Grease with a little butter and place a square of pastry in sandwich maker. Top with spoonfuls of filling and a square of pastry.

Brush the top square of pastry with a little butter and close lid. Cook for 4 to 5 minutes or until golden. Repeat with remaining pastry and filling.

SERVES 6

SHORTCRUST PASTRY

Shortcrust pastry is usually used for pies, tarts and slices. It is rich in vitamin A and iron.

Although it is easy to make, it is a lot more convenient to buy it from the supermarket frozen and ready rolled.

PEACH AND RASPBERRY TARTS

- *3 sheets ready-rolled puff pastry*
- *60 g (2 oz) butter*
- *4 tablespoons chopped roasted hazelnuts*
- *3 tablespoons sugar*
- *1 teaspoon ground cinnamon*
- *4 to 6 peaches, sliced*
- *185 g (6 oz) raspberries*
- *extra sugar*

Preheat oven to 220°C (425°F).

Cut each pastry sheet into 4 squares. With an 8 cm (3 in) pastry cutter cut the middle out of 6 pastry squares. Reserve middles for another recipe.

Lay 1 cut pastry square over a full square. Beat together butter, hazelnuts, sugar and cinnamon. Spread inside middle hole in pastry.

Top with slices of peach and raspberries. Sprinkle with extra sugar and place on baking trays. Bake for 12 to 15 minutes or until golden and crisp.

Cool, store and transport to your picnic in an airtight container.

MAKES 6

Fruit Strudel Jaffles

Packing a Picnic

For a purely portable picnic, the most versatile article you could buy is a picnic basket. Those with a lid are best — save those bottles rolling out as you walk down to the park!

These days picnic sets can be bought from homeware stores and department stores with the latest in picnic accessories. Non-breakable plates and cups come in a wide range of colours with cutlery to match.

A tablecloth is always a classy touch at a picnic — transport the dining room outside!

Something on the Side

Gone are the days of the limp lettuce leaf, sliced cucumber and tomato smothered with salad cream. The average supermarket, and of course the well-stocked vegetable market, provide a stunning array of vegetables and fruit which with imagination and experience can enhance any meal. Salads are limited only by your personal preferences, and to know that you are eating healthily is an added bonus.

Bowls from Country Road, fabric from Les Olivades

Salads

Salad making provides year-round opportunities for invention. Serve two or three with different dressings, or arrange prepared salad vegetables on large platters with separate bowls of mayonnaise or dressings so your guests can help themselves. Salads don't have to be served with the main meal. Use them as a starter on their own.

The amount of dressing doesn't need to double when you double the recipe. You only need a little dressing tossed through a salad to give it taste. Too much and everything will go soggy.

SALAD NIÇOISE

A slight twist on the traditional version.

> 150 g (6 oz) baby green beans, blanched
>
> 8 artichoke hearts, halved
>
> 75 g (3 oz) pitted black olives
>
> 2 tomatoes, cut into wedges
>
> 8 sun-dried tomatoes, halved
>
> 3 hard-boiled eggs, quartered
>
> 2 tablespoons shredded fresh basil

DRESSING

> 4 tablespoons olive oil
>
> 2 tablespoons balsamic vinegar
>
> 1 tablespoon grain mustard
>
> 2 tablespoons chopped fresh parsley

Arrange beans, artichokes, olives, tomatoes, eggs and basil on a serving platter.

To Prepare Dressing: Place oil, vinegar, mustard and parsley in a bowl and mix to combine. Pour over salad and toss lightly to combine. Chill until required.

SERVES 6

MIXED GREENS WITH BLUE BRIE DRESSING

Simple but delicious. For ideas on greens to use, see our salad greens identification picture on page 82. Use a variety of lettuces, endive and cress.

> 300g (10 oz) mixed salad greens

BLUE BRIE DRESSING

> 125 g (4 oz) blue brie
>
> 4 tablespoons olive oil
>
> 3 tablespoons natural yoghurt
>
> 1 tablespoon white wine vinegar
>
> 1 teaspoon cracked black pepper

Place greens in a serving bowl.

To Make Dressing: Place brie, oil, yoghurt, vinegar and pepper in a blender and blend until smooth.

Pour over salad greens and serve chilled.

SERVES 6

KING OF CAESAR SALAD

> 2 cos lettuce
>
> 6 rashers bacon, chopped
>
> 125 g (4 oz) croutons
>
> 250 g (8 oz) cherry tomatoes, halved
>
> 1 avocado, sliced

DRESSING

> ½ cup (125 ml/4 fl oz) olive oil
>
> 4 anchovies
>
> 2 cloves garlic, crushed
>
> 1 egg
>
> 2 teaspoons cracked black pepper
>
> 2 tablespoons fresh lemon juice
>
> 2 teaspoons wholegrain mustard
>
> 3 tablespoons raspberry or red wine vinegar
>
> ½ cup freshly shaved parmesan cheese

Break lettuce into large pieces and arrange on a serving platter. Sauté bacon until crisp and drain on absorbent paper. Add bacon to salad with croutons, tomatoes and avocado.

To Make Dressing: Place oil, anchovies, garlic, egg and pepper in a blender and blend until smooth. Gradually add lemon juice, mustard and vinegar. Pour dressing over salad, toss and top with parmesan cheese.

SERVES 6 TO 8

Picture previous pages: Left to right: King of Caesar Salad, Salad Niçoise (recipes page 72)

CITRUS MANGO SALAD

1 lettuce

3 oranges, peeled and segmented

3 stalks celery, sliced

2 mangoes, peeled and sliced

1 cucumber, sliced

6 spring onions, thinly sliced

DRESSING

3 tablespoons mayonnaise

4 tablespoons sour cream

2 tablespoons chopped fresh parsley

1 teaspoon French mustard

1 tablespoon fresh orange juice

2 teaspoons fresh lemon juice

Place lettuce, oranges, celery, mangoes, cucumber and spring onions on a serving platter.

Citrus Mango Salad

To Make Dressing: Place mayonnaise, sour cream, parsley, mustard and juices in a bowl and mix to combine.

Pour dressing over salad and serve chilled.

SERVES 6 TO 8

ROASTED VEGETABLE SALAD

1 large eggplant (aubergine), sliced lengthwise

salt

2 red capsicums (peppers), cut in half

olive oil

1 red onion, sliced

1 curly leaf lettuce

DRESSING

90 g (3 oz) soft blue vein cheese

1 tablespoon sour cream

3 tablespoons cream

2 tablespoons chopped fresh basil

Sprinkle eggplant slices with salt and allow to stand for 30 minutes. Wash and pat dry.

Place capsicum halves, skin side up, and eggplant under a hot grill. Brush well with oil. Grill capsicums until skin is charred and blistered. Remove skin and slice. Grill eggplant until golden on both sides.

Arrange eggplant, capsicums and onion over lettuce.

To Make Dressing: Combine cheese, sour cream, cream and basil. Pour over salad and chill until required.

SERVES 4

WARM SPINACH, ARTICHOKE AND PASTA SALAD

1 tablespoon olive oil

250 g (8 oz) button mushrooms, sliced

4 spring onions, sliced diagonally

1 bunch silver beet, washed and torn into pieces

170 g (5½ oz) jar marinated artichoke hearts

2 cups (300 g/10 oz) shell-shaped macaroni, cooked

3 tablespoons sun-dried tomatoes

4 tablespoons grated parmesan cheese

cracked black pepper

Heat oil in a pan and sauté mushrooms for 2 to 3 minutes. Stir through onions and silver beet and cook until just wilted.

Add undrained artichoke hearts and pasta and cook until heated through. Remove from heat and stir through tomatoes and parmesan. Season to taste with plenty of pepper and serve.

SERVES 6

PROSCIUTTO AND SUGAR PEA SALAD

3 tablespoons oil

12 slices prosciutto, cut into slivers

2 teaspoons butter

250 g (8 oz) sugar snap peas

1 butter lettuce, loosely torn

8 radicchio leaves

chives, snipped, to garnish

Heat oil in a small pan and sauté prosciutto in batches until crisp. Drain on absorbent paper.

Heat butter until foaming, add peas and toss until bright green in colour. Remove from heat and toss through lettuce, radicchio and prosciutto. Garnish with snipped chives.

SERVES 4

TROPICAL FRUITS WITH LEMON RIND DRESSING

3 mangoes, peeled

2 avocadoes, peeled

4 to 6 lettuce leaves

2 bananas, peeled and sliced lengthways

1½ cups (90 g/3 oz) shelled macadamia nuts, chopped

LEMON RIND DRESSING

1 teaspoon chopped lemon rind

1 tablespoon fresh lemon juice

2 tablespoons olive oil

2 tablespoons safflower oil

cayenne pepper, to taste

salt, to taste

Cut a thick slice lengthways down each side of the mango stone, then slice lenghways into 4 pieces. Slice avocadoes into 5 or 6 slices.

Place lettuce leaves on serving plates and arrange the mango, banana and avocado slices decoratively on top. Drizzle with Lemon Rind Dressing and sprinkle with macadamia nuts.

To Make Lemon Rind Dressing: Blend dressing ingredients well and let stand 5 to 10 minutes.

SERVES 4 TO 6

Roasted Vegetable Salad, Warm Spinach, Artichoke and Pasta Salad, Prosciutto and Sugar Pea Salad

Marinated Beef Salad

MARINATED BEEF SALAD

350 g (11 oz) sliced smoked beef

3 tablespoons fruity olive oil

½ cup (125 ml/4 fl oz) red wine vinegar

3 tablespoons honey

1 tablespoon fresh chopped mixed herbs

1 cucumber, peeled and sliced

½ cup (60 g/2 oz) pitted black olives

½ bunch curly endive

Place beef, oil, vinegar, honey and herbs in a small bowl. Cover and refrigerate for 1 hour.

Arrange beef, cucumber and olives on a bed of endive. Pour marinade over salad. Chill until required.

SERVES 6

WATERCRESS SALAD

1 bunch watercress

125 g (4 oz) mustard cress

½ bunch fresh spearmint, chopped

½ bunch chives, snipped

1 Spanish onion, sliced

1 avocado, peeled and sliced

DRESSING

1 tablespoon mayonnaise

2 tablespoons herb vinegar

1 teaspoon green peppercorns

2 tablespoons chopped parsley

4 tablespoons olive oil

Wash watercress thoroughly, and remove young tips. Discard stalks. Arrange watercress tips, mustard cress, spearmint, chives, onion and avocado in a large serving bowl.

To Make Dressing: Place mayonnaise, vinegar, peppercorns, parsley and oil in a small bowl and whisk to combine. Pour over salad just before serving.

SERVES 4

SPRING SALAD WITH CORIANDER DRESSING

1 small mignonette lettuce

1 witloof (Belgian endive, chicory)

100 g (3½ oz) rocket leaves

1 small bunch watercress

2 small radicchio

8 small nasturtium leaves

3 tablespoons chervil sprigs

3 tablespoons flat leafed parsley sprigs

1 green capsicum (pepper), sliced

250 g (8 oz) cherry tomatoes

CORIANDER DRESSING

2 teaspoons Dijon-style mustard

3 tablespoons fresh lemon juice

6 tablespoons olive oil

3 tablespoons chopped fresh coriander

Wash and dry all the salad leaves. Arrange them in a salad bowl with capsicum and tomatoes.

To Make Dressing: Place mustard and lemon juice in a small bowl. Whisk in oil until mixture thickens. Stir through coriander and serve over salad.

SERVES 6

ROASTED VEGETABLES WITH STILTON DRESSING

4 potatoes, cubed

1 sweet potato, cubed

500 g (1 lb) pumpkin, cubed

2 turnips, cubed

olive oil

3 sprigs rosemary

DRESSING

155 g (5 oz) stilton cheese

½ cup (125 ml/4 fl oz) natural yoghurt

1 tablespoon fresh lemon juice

1 teaspoon cracked black pepper

½ teaspoon ground cumin

Preheat oven to 200°C (400°F).

Place vegetables in a baking dish with oil and rosemary. Bake for 35 to 45 minutes or until cooked.

To Make Dressing: Place stilton, yoghurt, juice, pepper and cumin in a blender and blend until smooth. Pour over hot or warm vegetables.

SERVES 4 TO 6

RED CABBAGE SLAW WITH TAHINI ORANGE DRESSING

3 cups (270 g/9 oz) shredded red cabbage

1 cup (90 g/3 oz) shredded green cabbage

½ cup (155 g/5 oz) whole toasted blanched almonds

BASE DRESSING

2 tablespoons cream

1 tablespoon tarragon vinegar

1 teaspoon prepared mustard

¼ teaspoon salt

TAHINI ORANGE DRESSING

2 tablespoons tahini

2 tablespoons water

juice and finely grated rind 1 orange

Combine red and green cabbage, wash, drain and chill in refrigerator. To Make Base Dressing: Combine ingredients in a screwtop jar and shake well.

Toss cabbage with dressing and half the almonds. Pile into salad bowl and top remaining almonds.

To Make Tahini Orange Dressing: Combine ingredients and spoon over salad just before serving.

SERVES 6

NEW ITALIAN SALAD

- 1 curly endive
- 100 g (3 oz) rocket lettuce
- 185 g (6 oz) sun-dried capsicum (pepper), sliced
- 2 zucchini (courgettes), cut into ribbons
- 250 g (8 oz) baby bocconcini
- 3 tablespoons shredded purple basil
- 3 tablespoons olive oil
- 3 tablespoons balsamic vinegar
- 1 teaspoon cracked black pepper

Arrange endive, rocket, capsicums, zucchini, boconcini and basil on a serving plate.

Sprinkle with oil, vinegar and pepper. Cover, refrigerate and allow to stand for 1 hour before serving.

SERVES 6

ROASTED TOMATOES WITH PISTACHIO MINT PESTO

- 12 egg (Italian) tomatoes
- olive oil
- sea salt
- cracked black pepper

PISTACHIO MINT PESTO

- ½ cup (60 g/2 oz) pistachio nuts
- 40 g (1½ oz) mint leaves
- 2 cloves garlic, crushed
- ½ cup (30 g/1 oz) grated parmesan cheese
- 4 tablespoons olive oil

Preheat oven to 180°C (350°F).

Halve tomatoes lengthwise and place skin side down on a baking dish. Sprinkle with oil, salt and pepper. Bake for 30 minutes or until soft.

To Prepare Pesto: Place pistachios, mint, garlic, parmesan and oil in a blender and blend until very finely chopped. Serve with tomatoes.

SERVES 4 TO 6

AVOCADO AND LETTUCE SALAD WITH MUSTARD SEED DRESSING

- 2 avocadoes, peeled and sliced
- juice ½ lemon
- 1 lettuce
- 1 small cucumber, peeled and sliced
- 6 spring onions, finely chopped
- alfalfa sprouts

MUSTARD SEED DRESSING

- 2 tablespoons natural yoghurt
- 1 tablespoon vegetable oil
- 2 teaspoons mustard seeds
- 1 teaspoon grated ginger

Sprinkle lemon juice over avocado. Wash and dry lettuce. Refrigerate 30 minutes until crisp then tear into bite-sized pieces. Place in salad bowl. Top with avocado slices. Add cucumber and garnish with spring onions and alfalfa sprouts.

To Make Dressing: Combine all ingredients and mix until smooth. Just before serving, pour over salad and toss.

SERVES 8 TO 10

New Italian Salad, Roasted Tomatoes with Pistachio Mint Pesto

WHITE PLATE FROM PILLIVUYT, BLUE PLATE FROM ACCOUTREMENT, FABRIC FROM LES OLIVADES

SOMETHING ON THE SIDE 79

WARM SHREDDED CHICKEN SALAD

- 4 chicken breast fillets
- 1 tablespoon peanut oil
- 2 tablespoons chopped fresh coriander
- 2 tablespoon fresh lime or lemon juice
- ½ small cabbage, finely sliced
- 1 teaspoon sesame oil
- 2 tablespoons sesame seeds
- 8 radicchio leaves

Cut chicken into thin strips. Place in a bowl with oil, coriander and lime juice. Cover and stand for 20 minutes. Sauté in a hot pan for 4 minutes or until tender. Keep warm.

Sauté cabbage in sesame oil with the sesame seeds until wilted and tender.

Arrange radicchio on a serving platter. Top with sesame cabbage and chicken. Serve warm.

SERVES 4 TO 6

CARAMELISED SWEET POTATOES

- 3 sweet potatoes, cut into big pieces
- 6 baby onions, halved
- 6 cloves garlic
- 60 g (2 oz) butter, melted
- 90 g (3 oz) brown sugar
- 3 tablespoons water

Preheat oven to 180°C (350°F).

Place potato pieces in a baking dish with onions and garlic. Drizzle vegetables with butter, brown sugar and water. Bake for 30 minutes or until potatoes are soft and golden.

SERVES 6

THAI VEGETABLE SALAD

- 2 carrots, julienned
- 1 bunch asparagus, halved and lightly steamed
- 4 spring onions, sliced
- 8 stems English spinach, chopped
- 1 red capsicum (pepper), sliced

DRESSING

- 2 tablespoons chilli oil
- 2 teaspoons sesame oil
- 3 tablespoons rice vinegar
- 3 tablespoons tamari

Arrange carrot, asparagus, onions, spinach and capsicum on a serving platter.

To Make Dressing: Place oils, vinegar and tamari in a small bowl and whisk to combine. Pour over salad and serve chilled.

SERVES 4

LENTIL SALAD WITH YOGHURT DRESSING

- 1½ cups (300 g/10 oz) red lentils
- 2 cups (125 g/4 oz) chopped macadamia nuts
- ⅔ cup (90 g/3 oz) currants
- 4 spring onions, sliced
- 125 g (4 oz) mixed lettuce leaves

YOGHURT DRESSING

- 1 cup (250 ml/8 fl oz) natural yoghurt
- 2 tablespoons chopped fresh mint
- 1 clove garlic, crushed
- 2 tablespoons fresh lemon juice
- 2 tablespoons olive oil

Wash lentils until water runs clear. Simmer in a large pot of water for 15 minutes or until just soft, drain and cool.

Place lentils, nuts, currants, onions and lettuce in a bowl and mix to combine.

To Make Dressing: Place yoghurt, mint, garlic, lemon juice and oil in a small bowl and mix to combine. Pour over salad and serve chilled.

SERVES 4 TO 6

FENNEL AND ORANGE SALAD WITH TOMATO DRESSING

- 3 heads fennel
- 3 oranges
- 2 tablespoons chopped fresh parsley

TOMATO DRESSING

- 1 cup (250 ml/8 fl oz) tomato juice
- juice 1 lime or ½ lemon
- 2 spring onions, finely chopped
- 2 cloves garlic, chopped
- Worcestershire sauce, to taste
- Tabasco sauce, to taste
- freshly ground black pepper, to taste

Trim fennel, slice thinly; wash well and discard any discoloured slices. Cut both ends from oranges then cut off all rind and pith. With a small sharp knife, cut between membranes of oranges and free segments. Remove any seeds.

To Make Tomato Dressing: Combine all ingredients and mix thoroughly. Store in an airtight container in the refrigerator.

Combine oranges, fennel and Tomato Dressing. Cover, chill and serve sprinkled with parsley.

SERVES 10 TO 12

BARBECUED CHILLI CORN

6 corn cobs with husks

60 g (2 oz) butter, melted

1 teaspoon chilli powder

1 teaspoon ground cumin

1 teaspoon ground coriander

1 teaspoon cracked black pepper

Remove most of the husks from the corn. Use the remaining husks to wrap around the base of the corn as a handle.

Brush corn with combined butter, chilli, cumin, coriander and pepper. Barbecue until tender.

SERVES 6

Barbecued Chilli Corn

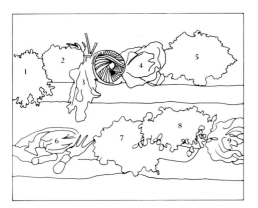

Salad Greens

1 Baby endive 2 Coral lettuce 3 Rocket leaves 4 Radicchio 5 Oak leaf 6 Cos lettuce 7 Red oak leaf 8 Watercress 9 Mignonette

Dash or Splash

*W*hy buy a dressing when it's so easy to make your own and you can create the exact flavour required? Once you've made a basic vinaigrette then you can make all kinds of combinations using herbs and spices of your choice.

Transform ordinary mayonnaise into a delicious dip or dressing, to serve with nibbles, salads and on sandwiches.

BASIC VINAIGRETTE

3 tablespoons white wine vinegar

½ cup (125 ml/4 fl oz) olive oil

1 teaspoon powdered mustard

freshly ground black pepper to taste

Place vinegar, oil, mustard and pepper in a screw top jar and shake well to combine. Store in refrigerator until required.

MAKES ½ CUP (125 ML/4 FL OZ)

HERB VINAIGRETTE

3 tablespoons white wine vinegar

½ cup (125 ml/4 fl oz) olive oil

1 teaspoon powdered mustard

freshly ground black pepper to taste

1 tablespoon chopped fresh chives

1 tablespoon chopped fresh basil

1 tablespoon chopped fresh parsley

Place vinegar, oil, mustard and pepper in a screw top jar and shake well to combine. Stir through herbs. Store in refrigerator until required.

MAKES ½ CUP (125 ML/4 FL OZ)

HERB MAYONNAISE

1 cup (250 ml/8 fl oz) mayonnaise

2 tablespoons chopped fresh parsley

2 tablespoons chopped fresh chives

2 tablespoons chopped fresh basil

2 teaspoons cracked black pepper

Place mayonnaise, parsley, chives, basil and pepper in a small bowl and mix well to combine. Store in an airtight container in refrigerator.

Serve over salads, vegetables or barbecued meats.

MAKES 1 CUP (250 ML/8 FL OZ)

CHILLI VINAIGRETTE

3 tablespoons white wine vinegar

½ cup (125 ml/4 fl oz) olive oil

1 teaspoon powdered mustard

freshly ground black pepper to taste

1 red chilli, seeded and finely chopped

1 tablespoon sweet chilli sauce

Place vinegar, oil, mustard and pepper in a screw top jar and shake well to combine. Shake through chilli and sweet chilli sauce. Store in refrigerator until required.

MAKES ½ CUP (125 ML/4 FL OZ)

RASPBERRY VINAIGRETTE

3 tablespoons raspberry vinegar

½ cup (125 ml/4 fl oz) olive oil

1 teaspoon powdered mustard

freshly ground black pepper to taste

Place vinegar, oil, mustard and pepper in a screw top jar and shake well to combine. Store in refrigerator until required.

MAKES ½ CUP (125 ML/4 FL OZ)

Making your own mayonnaise is too impractical for today's lifestyle. Good quality, ready-made mayonnaise is available in supermarkets and delicatessens. Use a good quality mayonnaise as a base for something more inspiring.

PESTO MAYONNAISE

- 1 cup (250 ml/8 fl oz) mayonnaise
- ½ cup (125 ml/4 fl oz) ready-made pesto
- 1 teaspoon cracked black pepper

Place mayonnaise, pesto and pepper in a small bowl and mix well to combine. Store in an airtight container in the refrigerator.

Serve over salads, vegetables or barbecued meats.

MAKES 1½ CUPS (375 ML/12 FL OZ)

TOMATO AND BASIL MAYONNAISE

- 1 cup (250 ml/8 fl oz) mayonnaise
- 2 tablespoons tomato paste
- 3 tablespoons chopped fresh basil
- 2 teaspoons cracked black pepper

Place mayonnaise, tomato, basil, and pepper in a small bowl and mix well to combine. Store in an airtight container in refrigerator.

Serve with salads, vegetables or barbecued meats.

MAKES 1 CUP (250 ML/8 FL OZ)

SWEET CURRY MAYONNAISE

- 1 cup (250 ml/8 fl oz) mayonnaise
- 1 tablespoon ground cumin
- 1 teaspoon ground chilli
- 2 tablespoons chopped fresh coriander
- 2 teaspoons curry powder
- 1 tablespoon brown sugar

Place mayonnaise, cumin, chilli, coriander, curry powder and brown sugar in a small bowl and mix to combine. Store in an airtight container in refrigerator.

Serve over salads, vegetables or barbecued meats.

MAKES 1 CUP (250 ML/8 FL OZ)

HERBED YOGHURT DRESSING

- 1 cup (250 ml/8 fl oz) low-fat natural yoghurt
- 2 tablespoons chopped fresh parsley
- 1 tablespoon snipped fresh chives
- 1 tablespoon prepared mustard
- salt and freshly ground black pepper

Combine yoghurt, herbs and seasoning in a bowl. Store in an airtight container and refrigerate before using. Use as needed.

MAKES 1 CUP (250 ML/8 FL OZ)

Almond, hazelnut and walnut oil have a good nutty flavour that complements many salads. Polyunsaturated oils such as corn oil, peanut oil, safflower oil and sunflower oil are light with little flavour and may be used in combination with one of the more full-bodied oils to lighten a particular dressing. Used alone they tend to lack flavour. Grapeseed oil is light and has a good nutty flavour. Olive oil is the most widely used and has a full flavour and smoothness that it very versatile. Extra virgin oil is the best. Sesame oil has a strong sesame flavour. Use sparingly as it can overpower the salad.

Make your own chilli oil: Warm 2 cups (500 ml/16 fl oz) olive oil and pour into a clean bottle with 1 to 2 teaspoons chopped red chillies. Cap and store in a cool, dark place for 2 weeks.

Make your own herb-infused oil: Warm 2 cups (500 ml/16 fl oz) olive oil and pour into a clean jar with ¼ cup fresh herbs. Cover and leave for 2 weeks. Strain the oil through a fine cheesecloth into a bottle and store in a cool, dark place until required.

From left to right: Raspberry Vinaigrette, Chilli Vinaigrette, Herb Vinaigrette, Herb Mayonnaise, Tomato and Basil Mayonnaise

Salad Vegetables

Name	Description
Alfalfa sprouts	Sold in punnets or loose and eaten at the seedling stage when full of vitamins and minerals.
Artichoke hearts	Sold in oil in jars, or canned in brine.
Artichokes (globe or common)	Artichokes make a good container for an individual salad. They resemble an unopened flower bud with tightly wrapped leaves.
Asparagus	Young shoot of a green plant. A popular addition to salads.
Avocado	This pear-shaped fruit has a delicate yet very distinctive flavour. Skin colour varies from green to black depending on variety.
Baby squash	Eaten when very young and tender. Green or yellow in colour. Similar in flavour to a baby zucchini.
Beans	Green, crisp pods with flavoursome seeds.
Bean sprouts	These are sprouted mung beans used when the sprout is about 3 cm long. Should be crisp and sweet-smelling when purchased.
Chinese cabbage	Elongated cabbage with green-edged leaves. Heart nearly white.
Red cabbage	Round cabbage, deep red leaves.
Round head cabbage	Smooth pale green leaves.
Savoy cabbage	Has dark green wrinkled leaves with a firmly packed head.
White cabbage	Round, tight head.
Capsicum (pepper)	May be green, red, yellow or black. The sweet peppery flavour is very distinctive.
Carrots	Use young, crisp carrots for salads.
Cauliflower	Tight head of white flower buds.

Storage	Preparation
Keep refrigerated as they continue to grow.	Simply pull required amount from punnet.
Refrigerate after opening.	Delightful sliced into a salad.
Refrigerate in a plastic bag for up to 7 days.	Pull off any coarse outer leaves. Cut off top third of the artichoke. Remove hairy choke and cook in boiling, salted water (made slightly acidic with a dash of vinegar or squeeze of lemon juice) for 20–40 minutes, depending on their size. Cool and serve filled with a vinaigrette dressing or fill with a salad of your choice.
Refrigerate in a plastic bag for 2 to 3 days.	Blanch in boiling, salted water and refresh before using or simply steam lightly. May be used whole if young, or cut into spears.
Store at room temperature until ripe then refrigerate for up to 3 days.	Eat at room temperature for full flavour. Slice just before using — otherwise rub the cut surfaces with lemon juice or vinaigrette.
Refrigerate for a few days.	Steam or stir fry before using in salads.
Refrigerate in a plastic bag for up to 5 days.	Crisp, young green runner beans need only topping, tailing and rinsing before use. May be sliced or left whole.
Refrigerate for up to 7 days.	Pinch off the dry, stringy end of the root before using.
Refrigerate in a plastic bag for up to 7 days.	Crinkly leaves may be shredded and used raw.
Refrigerate in a plastic bag for up to 7 days.	Usually cooked with vinegar. May be finely shredded for coleslaw, adding a beautiful, purple-red colour to the slaw.
Refrigerate in a plastic bag for up to 7 days.	Shred and use in coleslaw or steam and use in other salads.
Refrigerate in a plastic bag for up to 7 days.	Good shredded in coleslaw.
Refrigerate in a plastic bag for up to 7 days.	Usually used shredded for coleslaw or sauerkraut.
Refrigerate in crisper for up to 10 days.	Use raw or char skin and use cooked. Halve, remove seeds and woody stem. Slice or chop.
Refrigerate in a plastic bag with paper towel for up to 7 days.	Peel if necessary. Grate, julienne or leave whole if very small.
Remove tough leaves and refrigerate in crisper for up to 5 days.	For salads, break into florets and blanch in boiling salted water. Drain and refresh under cold, running water and dry well.

Salad Vegetables (continued)

Name	Description
Celery	Sold in whole or half heads. Leaf and stem both edible.
Cucumbers	
Apple	Small, creamy white and oval-shaped.
Green or ridge	Smooth-skinned and dark green.
Lebanese	Small, smooth-skinned green cucumber.
Telegraph	A long, thin, dark green variety of cucumber, crisp with a good flavour.
Garlic	Choose firm, young white or purple bulbs when purchasing.
Kohlrabi	A cabbage–turnip type of vegetable, wether purple or green in colour. The thickened stem is eaten and has a delicate turnip flavour.
Mushrooms	Use firm, white button mushrooms or caps in a salad.
Onions	
Shallot (scallion, sometimes called green onions)	Fresh onion flavour.
Spring onion	These have a white bulb with long green tops. Sold in bunches. Mild onion flavour.
Spanish onion	Mild, sweet juicy onion with a red colour which makes an attractive addition to salads.
True French shallot	Small brownish bulb with a mild onion flavour.
White onions	Round, firm and white-fleshed with a dry white papery skin.
Radish	Firm, crisp, red bulbs, sold in bunches. Tops should be fresh-looking.
Snake beans	Long, round-bodied thin bean. Similar in taste and texture to green bean. Sold in bunches.
Tomatoes	Always use tomatoes at room temperature. Look for a good red colour and firm flesh when using in salads. Whole cherry tomatoes or tom thumbs are a welcome addition to any salad. Also available are the small, yellow pear-shaped tomatoes, which have a surprisingly good flavour.

Storage	Preparation
Refrigerate in a plastic bag for up to 7 days.	May be sliced or cut into sticks. For celery curls, split 6 cm lengths halfway down each piece a few times. Repeat at other end and plunge into iced water. Leave until curled and crisp.
Wash and dry, store in crisper in refrigerator for up to 7 days.	Peel before using.
Wash and dry, store in crisper in refrigerator for up to 7 days.	Peel, leaving a little of the green skin (this is said to help with digestion). The surface may be scored with a fork. May be sliced into rounds or halved and seeded then sliced. Some people still like to lightly salt the slices to remove indigestible juices. Allow to stand for 30 minutes, drain and rinse will with cold water.
Wash and dry, store in crisper in refrigerator for up to 7 days.	Chop and use in salads.
Wash and dry, store in crisper in refrigerator for up to 7 days.	Chop and use in salads.
Keep in a dry, airy place or peel cloves and keep in a jar of oil in the refrigerator.	Remove papery skin by crushing clove with back of a knife. Continue crushing and add a pinch salt. The salt acts as an abrasive to pulp the flesh while also absorbing pungent juices. Use a garlic press to crush if you prefer.
Refrigerate in a crisper for up to 7 days.	May be boiled or eaten raw. Add to salads grated or sliced. Delicious offset by horseradish.
Refrigerate unwashed in a brown paper bag for up to 7 days.	Brush off any compost (don't rinse) and trim stalk end. Serve whole or sliced.
Refrigerate in a crisper.	Trim away roots and peel dry outer leaves before using.
Refrigerate in a crisper.	Use white bulb with a little of the green stem finely chopped.
Refrigerate in a crisper.	Peel outer leaves, chop or slice and add to salad.
Refrigerate in a crisper.	Used mainly in sautés.
Store in a cool, dry, dark place.	Peel before use. Strong, hot, pungent flavour. Use sparingly.
Remove leaves, refrigerate in a plastic bag for up to 7 days.	Slice or serve whole with a few small, green sprigs still attached. Remove stringy root.
Loosely wrap and refrigerate for up to 7 days.	Slice and blanch before using in a salad.
Store at room temperature out of direct sunlight until ripe, then refrigerate for up to 5 days only.	Wash and dry. Slice or quarter for use in salads. Use cherry tomatoes whole.

Salad Greens

Name	Description	Flavour
Chicory (Belgian endive or whitloof)	Tightly clustered, smooth white leaves with yellow tips.	Slightly bitter
Curly endive	Sold in large bunches. The long leaves graduate from pale, greeny yellow to dark green. Use only the paler heart and stalks.	Bitter
Escarole	Long frilly leaves. Use only the centre young leaves.	Slightly bitter
Butter lettuce (round lettuce)	Soft, smallish lettuce.	Mild
Cos or Romaine lettuce	Elongated head of dark green oval leaves and a crisp pale green heart.	Has a pungent flavour and stays crisp
Iceberg or crisp head lettuce	A large lettuce with crisp outer leaves and a firm sweet heart. This is the basis of many a salad as the leaves will stay crisp.	Sweet heart, stays crisp
Mignonette lettuce	Soft, smallish leaves with edges tinged pink to red.	Slightly bitter
Mustard and cress	Seeds are usually sown together and eaten at the seedling stage. Sold in punnets. Snip off the tops as required.	Hot and peppery
Radicchio	Sold as tiny, single loose leaves either wholly green or tinged with red. Some varieties come as a slightly conical head.	Slightly bitter
Rocket	Small, acidic, dark green leaves. Sold while the plant is still very young.	Acidic
Silver beet	Often called spinach, beet or chard. Used in salads only when leaves are very young. Discard the white stalk. The older, larger leaves should be steamed and eaten hot.	Mild
Spinach (English)	Dark green leaves. Eaten raw in salads when leaves are young and fresh. Stalk may be eaten as well.	Mild
Watercress	Pick over the bunch using only young leaves and tender stems for salads. Whatever remains will make an excellent soup.	Pungent, slightly peppery

Oven temperatures

Temperatures	Celsius (°C)	Fahrenheit (°F)	Gas Mark
Very slow	120	250	½
Slow	150	300	2
Moderately slow	160-180	325-350	3-4
Moderate	190-200	375-400	5-6
Moderately hot	220-230	425-450	7
Hot	250-260	475-500	8-9

NOTE: We developed the recipes in this book in Australia where the tablespoon measure is 20 ml. In many other countries the tablespoon is 15 ml. For most recipes this difference will not be noticeable.

However, for recipes using baking powder, gelatine, bicarbonate of soda, small amounts of flour and cornflour, we suggest people outside Australia add an extra teaspoon for each tablespoon specified.

Glossary of Terms

Australia	UK	USA
beetroot	beetroot	beet
black olive	black olive	ripe olive
blade steak	shoulder or chuck steak	blade/chuck steak
broad bean	broad bean	fava bean
butternut pumpkin		butternut squash/summer squash
calamari	squid	calamari
capsicum	pepper	sweet pepper
chicken breasts fillets	chicken breast fillets	boneless chicken breasts
chickpea	chickpea	garbanzo bean
chilli	chilli	chili
chump chop (lamb)	chump chop	leg chop
coriander (fresh)	coriander/Indian parsley	cilantro/Chinese parsley
cornflour	cornflour	cornstarch
cornmeal/polenta	polenta/maize meal	cornmeal
cream	single cream	light cream
dill	dill	dill weed
eggplant	aubergine	eggplant
fish cutlet	fish cutlet	fish steak
frying pan	frying pan	skillet
green cabbage	white or roundhead cabbage	cabbage
grill	grill	broil
natural yoghurt	natural yoghurt	unflavoured yoghurt
paper towel	absorbent kitchen paper	paper towel
pawpaw	papaya	papaya or pawpaw
pine nut	pine nut	pignolias
plain flour	(general purpose) flour	all-purpose flour
pork fillet	pork fillet	pork tenderloin
prawn	prawn or shrimp	prawn
rasher (bacon)	rasher	slice
rump steak	rump steak	sirloin
shallots	spring onions	scallions/green onions
shin (of beef)		shank
silver beet (spinach)	silver beet (chard)	Swiss chard
snow pea	mangetout, sugar pea	snow pea
stock cube	stock cube	bouillon cube
tomato paste	tomato purée	tomato paste
tomato purée	tomato purée	tomato paste
topside beef	topside beef	round beef
topside steak		round steak
zucchini	courgette	zucchini

Index

Asparagus and gorgonzola
    slice 54
Avocado
    butter 15
    and lettuce salad with
      mustard seed dressing 79

Balmain bugs with lime and
    coriander butter 26
Balsamic smoked beef
    rounds 15
Beef
    balsamic smoked beef
      rounds 15
    barbecued, warm salad
      with radicchio 37
    barbecued fillet, with
      horseradish cream 31
    char-grilled, with avocado
      and tomatoes 25
    glazed sirloins 31
    Italian roulade 64
    sage and onion rolls 64
    salad, marinated 76
    spicy skewered meatballs 13
Blue brie dressing 72
Bocconcini, marinated 23
Bread, recipes for making
    buttermilk 49
    cheese and bacon 51
    damper 48
    fruit and tea damper 48
Bread, recipes using
    see also Spreads
    bruschetta 19
    cheese and chive 49
    cheese and olive melts 17
    flat bread with sesame
      topping 47
    French onion 51
    garlic and herb 49
    ham and blue cheese 49
    patafla 51
    picnic loaf 60
    sand-wedges 60
    smoked chicken focaccia 54
    smoked salmon sandwiches
      55
Brochettes, Greek 25
Bruschetta 19
Butter
    avocado 15
    chilli 47
    clarified 19

lime and coriander 26
    mustard pepperoni 47
    pecorino herb 47
    salmon and dill 47
Buttermilk bread 49

Caesar salad 72
Cajun blackened chicken 32
Cake, tangelo syrup 56
Capsicum
    dip 22
    and mushroom 19
Caramelised sweet potatoes 80
Cheese
    and bacon loaf 51
    blue brie dressing 72
    chive and pecan rounds 10
    and chive bread 49
    marinated bocconcini 23
    and olive melts 17
    oyster puffs 10
    pecorino herb butter 47
    and port spread 10
    and spinach pastries 63
    spread 60
    stilton dressing 77
    zucchini and fetta 19
Chicken
    barbecued oregano 32
    cajun blackened 32
    pear and blue brie 33
    peppered paté 19
    sesame drumsticks 22
    smoked, focaccia of 54
    with spicy pecan stuffing
      36
    tandoori 28
    Thai, with potato
      pancakes 40
    warm shredded salad 80
Chilli
    barbecue spare ribs 36
    butter 47
    corn 81
    meat pastries 63
    pepper yabbies 38
    vinaigrette 84
Chive and pecan cheese
    rounds 10
Chocolate nut slice 67
Citrus mango salad 73
Clarified butter 19
Coconut
    cookies 56
    coriander salsa 42
    curry puffs 12
Cod, lemon and pepper 31

Cookies, coconut rough 56
Coriander dressing 77
Corn, barbecued chilli 81
Cream cheese pastries 63
Curry
    coconut puffs 12
    mayonnaise 85

Damper 48
    fruit and tea 48
Desserts
    baby lemon meringue
      pies 56
    fruit strudel jaffles 67
    peach and raspberry tarts
      67
    tangelo syrup cake 56
Dip, roasted capsicum 22
Dressing
    see also Mayonnaise;
      Vinaigrette
    blue brie 72
    coriander 77
    herbed yoghurt 85
    lemon rind 74
    mustard seed 79
    stilton 77
    tahini orange 77
    tomato 80
    yoghurt 80

Fennel and orange salad with
    tomato dressing 80
Fetta and zucchini 19
Fish
    see also Salmon
    Italian parcels 28
    kebabs 26
    lemon and pepper cod 31
    red mullet in corn husks
      34
    salt baked 36
    smoked trout tartlets 17
    steaks 36
Flat bread with sesame
    topping 47
Focaccia, smoked chicken 54
French onion loaf 51
Fruit strudel jaffles 67
Fruit and tea damper 48

Garlic and herb bread 49
Ghee 19
Glazed sirloins 31
Greek brochettes 25

Ham
    and blue cheese bread 49
    and mushroom pastries 15
Herb
    mayonnaise 84
    pancakes with avocado
      butter 15
    vinaigrette 84
    yoghurt dressing 85
Hollandaise, lime 34
Honey lamb skewers 26
Honeyed prawns 20
Horseradish cream 31

Italian beef roulade 64
Italian fish parcels 28
Italian salad 79

Jaffles, fruit strudel 67

Kebabs
    fish 26
    honey lamb 26
    spicy skewered meatballs 13
King of Caesar salad 72

Lamb
    Greek brochettes 25
    honey skewers 26
    minted burgers 29
    Moroccan fillets 42
    spicy barbecued leg 42
    tandoori cutlets 38
Lemon
    meringue pies 56
    and pepper cod 31
Lemon rind dressing 74
Lentil salad with yoghurt
    dressing 80
Lime
    and coriander butter 26
    hollandaise 34
    and pepper prawns 26
Lobster
    with cress and balsamic
      vinegar 39
    with macadamias 38

Mango salsa 40
Mayonnaise
    herb 84
    pesto 20, 85
    sweet curry 85
    tomato and basil 85
Meatballs, spicy skewered 13

Minced beef
    sage and onion rolls 64
    spicy skewered meatballs 13
Minted lamb burgers 29
Mixed greens with blue brie
    dressing 72
Moroccan lamb fillets 42
Mullet in corn husks 34
Mushroom
    and capsicum 19
    and ham pastries 15
    and roasted pepper
        risotto 55
Mustard pepperoni butter 47
Mustard seed dressing 79

Octopus, char-grilled, with
    pesto mayonnaise 20
Onion loaf 51
Orange tahini dressing 77
Oysters
    cheese puffs 10
    Mediterranean 20

Pancakes
    herb, with avocado butter
        15
    potato 40
Pasta, warm summer 55
Pastries, savoury
    coconut curry puffs 12
    mushroom and herb 15
    pocket 63
Patafla 51
Paté
    peppered chicken 19
    pork and veal terrine 61
    salmon and lime 12
Peach and raspberry tarts 67
Pear and blue brie chicken 33
Pecan stuffing 36
Pecorino and herb butter 47
Peppered chicken paté 19
Pesto
    mayonnaise 20, 85
    pistachio mint 79
Pies, dessert: lemon
    meringue 56
Pies, savoury: sesame cheese
    60
Pistachio mint pesto 79
Pocket pastries 63
Pork
    chilli barbecue spare ribs 36
    and nectarine rolls 38
    prosciutto wrapped fillets 40
    and veal terrine 61

Potato
    and bacon salad 60
    pancakes 40
Prawns
    and cheese tarts 63
    with creamy cashew sauce
        16
    with creamy satay sauce 28
    crispy, with mango salsa 40
    honeyed 20
    lime and pepper 26
Prosciutto
    and sugar pea salad 74
    wrapped pork fillets 40

Raspberry vinaigrette 84
Ratatouille tart 55
Red cabbage slaw with tahini
    orange dressing 77
Red mullet in corn husks 34
Ricotta cheese sesame pie 60
Risotto, mushroom and
    roasted pepper 55
Roasted capsicum dip 22
Roasted vegetable salad 74
Roasted vegetables with
    stilton dressing 77
Roulade, Italian beef 64

Sage and onion rolls 64
Salad
    see also Warm salad
    avocado and lettuce, with
        mustard seed dressing 79
    citrus mango 73
    fennel and orange, with
        tomato dressing 80
    Italian 79
    king of Caesar 72
    lentil, with yoghurt
        dressing 80
    marinated beef 76
    mixed greens, with blue
        brie dressing 72
    niçoise 72
    potato and bacon 60
    prosciutto and sugar pea
        74
    red cabbage slaw with
        tahini orange dressing 77
    roasted tomatoes with
        pistachio mint pesto 79
    roasted vegetable 74
    roasted vegetables with
        stilton dressing 77
    spring, with coriander
        dressing 77

Thai vegetable 80
    tropical fruits, with
        lemon rind dressing 74
    watercress 77
Salmon
    and chive log 12
    with coconut coriander
        salsa 42
    and dill butter 47
    and lime paté 12
    smoked, sandwiches of 17
Salsa
    coconut coriander 42
    mango 40
Salt baked fish 36
Sand-wedges 60
Sandwiches
    sand-wedges 60
    smoked salmon 54
Sauce
    see also Dressing; Salsa
    horseradish cream 31
    lime hollandaise 34
    pistachio mint pesto 79
Scallops, char-grilled, with
    lime hollandaise 34
Seafood
    see also Lobster; Oysters;
        Prawns
    Balmain bugs with lime
        and coriander butter 26
    char-grilled baby octopus
        with pesto mayonnaise
        20
    char-grilled scallops with
        lime hollandaise 34
    chilli pepper yabbies 38
    pastries 63
Sesame cheese pie 60
Sesame drumsticks 22
Slaw, red cabbage, with
    tahini orange dressing 77
Slice, chocolate nut 67
Smoked beef balsamic
    rounds 15
Smoked chicken focaccia 54
Smoked salmon sandwiches
    55
Smoked trout tartlets 17
Spare ribs, chilli barbecue 36
Spinach
    artichoke and pasta warm
        salad 74
    tortilla 60
Spreads
    see also Butter
    cheese and port 10

Spring salad with coriander
    dressing 77
Stacked picnic loaf 60
Steak see Beef
Stilton dressing 77
Stuffing, pecan 36
Sweet potatoes, caramelised
    80

Tahini orange dressing 77
Tandoori
    chicken 28
    lamb cutlets 38
Tangelo syrup cake 56
Tarts, dessert: peach and
    raspberry 67
Tarts, savoury
    prawn and cheese 63
    ratatouille 55
    smoked trout 17
Terrine, pork and veal 61
Thai chicken with potato
    pancakes 40
Thai vegetable salad 80
Tomatoes
    and basil mayonnaise 85
    dressing 80
    roasted, with pistachio
        mint pesto 79
    sage, and red onion 19
Tortilla, spinach 60
Tropical fruits with lemon
    rind dressing 74
Trout, smoked, tartlets of 17

Veal with sweet potato
    rounds 40
Vinaigrette
    basic recipe 84
    chilli 84
    herb 84
    raspberry 84

Warm salad
    barbecued beef and
        radicchio 37
    shredded chicken 80
    spinach, artichoke and
        pasta 74
Watercress salad 77

Yabbies, chilli pepper 38
Yoghurt
    dressing 80
    and herb dressing 85

Zucchini and fetta 19

ENJOY A WORLD OF GOOD COOKING WITH THE
BAY BOOKS COOKERY COLLECTION

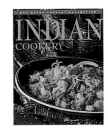

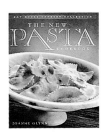

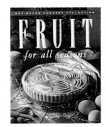
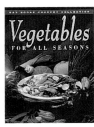

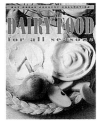
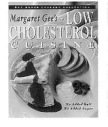

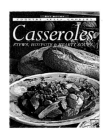

If these titles are not available from your regular stockists, please contact the HarperCollins Sales Office in your State:

WESTERN AUSTRALIA	SOUTH AUSTRALIA	QUEENSLAND	VICTORIA	NEW SOUTH WALES
SUITE 2 , 25 BELGRAVIA ST	UNIT 1 , 1-7 UNION ST	643 KESSELS ROAD	22-24 JOSEPH STREET	25 RYDE ROAD
BELMONT WA 6104	STEPNEY SA 5069	UPPER MOUNT GRAVATT	NORTH BLACKBURN	PYMBLE NSW 2073
TEL: (09) 479 4988	TEL: (08) 363 0122	QLD 4122	VIC 3130	TEL: (02) 952 5000
FAX: (09) 478 3248	FAX: (08) 363 1653	TEL: (07) 849 7855	TEL: (03) 895 8100	FAX: (02) 952 5777
		FAX: (07) 349 8286	FAX: (03) 895 8199	